I0014954

# Scrum in AI

Artificial Intelligence Agile
Development with Scrum and MLOps

Paolo Sammicheli

# Scrum in AI

## Artificial Intelligence Agile Development with Scrum and MLOps

Paolo Sammicheli

ISBN 9798711928454

This work is licensed under a Creative Commons Attribution-ShareAlike 4.0 International License

# Tweet This Book!

Please help Paolo Sammicheli by spreading the word about this book on Twitter!

The suggested hashtag for this book is #scrum-ai.

Find out what other people are saying about the book by clicking on this link to search for this hashtag on Twitter:

#scrum-ai

# Contents

Dedication      iii

Acknowledgements      v

Foreword      vii

Introduction to the printed version      xi

Why AI and Agile?      xiii

Open-Source Agile Publication      xv

Introducing myself      xix

## Fundamentals      1

Artificial Intelligence      3

Agile      19

Scrum      29

Scrum Patterns      43

Open and Inner Source      53

# In Practice 83

Scrum in Artificial Intelligence 85

Engineering Practices 93

Project Chartering 109

Product Backlog Creation 113

Multiple Teams 127

Going into Production 155

# Coaching Conversations 169

Animal Health Application 171

Rasa.com 177

Tiledesk.com 181

# Appendix 187

Popcorn Flow 189

Cynefin 197

Agile Management 203

How to interview the Scrum Master 207

Electronic Version 213

This page intentionally left blank

# Dedication

To Jeff, Arline, JJ, Jessica,
and all the folks at Scrum Inc.

Infinite gratitude for all the support, learning, and fun.

Dedication

# Acknowledgements

This book wouldn't exist if my business partner Alessandro weren't supporting me like he always did. At the pandemic's beginning, I expressed the desire to return to school to improve myself. And I was attracted by the vast MIT Sloan Executive Education[1] offer. He said "yes" immediately, even if the cost was high and we were at the beginning of a period that would have been economically challenging. That created the spark that boosted my interest in Artificial Intelligence.

The ultimate fuel that allowed this project to liftoff was the immediate support and encouragement from the Sutherland family, Jessica Larsen, and all the folks at Scrum Inc[2].

A huge thanks go to Fabio Colinelli[3], who designed the book's cover; Having the cover ready since the first iterations helped me picture the final result in my mind.

Last but not least, I would like to thank all my friends and colleagues who contributed to this book in different ways.

[1]https://exec.mit.edu

[2]https://www.scruminc.com

[3]An interview with the cover's author is available here: https://www.scrum-ai.com/blog/the-design-on-the-cover-is-awesome-who-s-the-artist

# Foreword

The second person to adopt Scrum for his company was Mike Beedle in 1994. He had been following the creation of Scrum in the internet newsgroups and said, "I get it, it is all based on AI!" Mike had a doctoral degree in Artificial Intelligence. He was later a Signatory of the Agile Manifesto and wrote the first book on Scrum with Ken Schwaber, Agile Software Development with Scrum[4].

In 1970, the U.S. Air Force sent me to Stanford University to get a Master's Degree in Statistics and I spent a third of my time for the next two years programming in LISP at the Stanford Artificial Intelligence Laboratory (SAIL). John McCarthy was the Director of the Lab and one of the founders of the discipline of artificial intelligence[5].[6] He co-authored the document that coined the term "artificial intelligence" (AI), developed the Lisp[7] programming language[8] family, significantly influenced the design of the ALGOL[9] programming language, popularized time-sharing[10], and invented garbage collection[11]. He would come by my workstation about every other day complaining bitterly that I was using 10% of the entire compute power of the Lab on developing my smart chess program, but he never stopped me from working in the Lab.

Fast forward to 1984 and I am in Marvin Minsky's lab at MIT as part of a Kellogg Fellowship program educating other Fellows on AI. In the corner there was a long-haired programmer. I went over

---

[4]https://www.goodreads.com/book/show/55645252-agile-software-development-with-scrum-series-in-agile-software-developm

[5]https://en.wikipedia.org/wiki/Artificial_intelligence

[6]https://en.wikipedia.org/wiki/John_McCarthy_(computer_scientist)#cite_note-1

[7]https://en.wikipedia.org/wiki/Lisp_(programming_language)

[8]https://en.wikipedia.org/wiki/Programming_language

[9]https://en.wikipedia.org/wiki/ALGOL

[10]https://en.wikipedia.org/wiki/Time-sharing

[11]https://en.wikipedia.org/wiki/Garbage_collection_(computer_science)

and asked him what he was doing and he said he was writing a free operating system, compilers, editors, everything that was needed and launched into a long rant on how all software should be free. This was Richard Stallman, founder of the Free Software Foundation, creation of GNU, Emacs, and many free software tools, later a MacArthur Fellow and winner of many of the most prestigious awards in computer science.

By 1986, inspired by Minsky and Stallman, I had engineered my way into a CTO job down the street from the MIT AI Lab, was working with other AI researchers, co-founded Individual Inc based on the SMART linguistical analysis and documentation retrieval system from Cornell, and in 1988 joined Graphael, a LISP Object Database company. In 1989, I moved the company into a startup building to fill space vacated by Symbolics, one of the first successful LISP machine companies.

Professor Rodney Brooks and his graduate students at the MIT AI Lab came down the street to visit my company and asked if they could rent some of my lab space to start up iROBOT[12]. Their autonomous robot, Ghengis Kahn[13], built on Brooks subsumption architecture, was a model of how to use simple rules to quickly evolve a smart autonomous system. Similar rules were used to create the first Scrum team in 1993.

Genghis Kahn[14] now is in the National Air and Space Museum[15] of

---

[12]https://www.irobot.com
[13]https://robots.ieee.org/robots/genghis/
[14]Pictures from the MIT Computer Science & Artificial Intelligence Lab: http://www.ai.mit.edu/projects/genghis/genghis.html
[15]https://en.wikipedia.org/wiki/National_Air_and_Space_Museum

the Smithsonian Institution[16].

When I was immersed in studying neural networks and genetic algorithms in 1987, a paper by Christopher Langdon was published out of the Santa Fe Institute mathematically demonstrating that evolution proceeds most quickly as a system is made flexible to the edge of chaos. This demonstrated that confusion and struggle was essential to emerging peak performance (of people, or software architectures, both of which are journeys though an evolutionary design space). It also showed clearly why waterfall projects slow down as you add people, methodologies, roles, meetings, and reports.

Increasing the degrees of freedom of the team to the edge of chaos and not beyond emerged from AI and is at the root of Scrum. To this day my partner, Ken Schwaber, calls his early resource web site controlchaos.com[17]. You can read about some of this early influence at Nativity Scene: How Scrum was Born![18]

Because Scrum emerged from a hotbed of AI concepts, implementations, and companies, it is with great pleasure that I recommend reading this new book from one of the best Scrum trainers in the world, Paolo Sammicheli. His keen insight into the topic and his ability to show how Scrum can produce better AI solutions brings the relationship between Scrum and AI full circle into contemporary times. It was more than 30 years ago that Christopher Langdon mathematically proved that complex adaptive systems simulated on the computer evolve more quickly as they approach the edge of chaos – the basis for team autonomy in Scrum.

**Jeff Sutherland**
Inventor and co-author of Scrum

---

[16]https://en.wikipedia.org/wiki/Smithsonian_Institution
[17]http://www.controlchaos.com
[18]https://www.scruminc.com/nativity-scene-how-scrum-was-born/

# Introduction to the printed version

What you're now holding in your hands is not my book. I'm not trying to imitate René Magritte[19] with his "Ceci n'est pas une pipe[20]" painting. What I mean is that what you're holding in your hand is a picture of a living thing that is growing continuously. What you bought, in reality, is lifetime access to the electronic version of this book. On the last page, you'll find the link and the QRCode to download it for free on Leanpub and receive updates forever.

Even if you're the kind who loves to read paper books rather than ebooks, I recommend downloading the electronic version before starting to read it. Some pictures, especially screenshots, contain many details you would want to zoom in on a big computer screen. If you have questions or want to suggest improvements drop me a message on my website: https://paolo.sammiche.li/contact

I wish you a good reading and a pleasant learning experience.

---

[19]https://en.wikipedia.org/wiki/René_Magritte
[20]https://en.wikipedia.org/wiki/The_Treachery_of_Images

# Why AI and Agile?

Why this book? In my entire career, I just surpassed 30 years, I rarely found something desperately needing a well-implemented Scrum like Artificial Intelligence development. And besides this, I encounter companies and well-paid consultants using old Waterfall tools to inflict detailed analysis and rigorous planning on their AI development groups. And the worse are the so-called "Agile Zealots[21]." They apply the Agile Practices with bureaucratic rigor instead of relying on Principles. According to Jeff Sutherland, the co-author of Scrum and the Agile Manifesto, "the enemy of Scrum is not Waterfall, is bad Scrum" because this is damaging the Scrum and Agile reputation.

With this book, I want to contribute to the spread of Scrum: a lightweight approach that was never meant to be religiously followed and bureaucratized by consultants and experts like, unfortunately, is happening these days.

I hope this book will be a breath of fresh air for those overwhelmed by rigid practices and useless meetings.

---

[21]https://en.wikipedia.org/wiki/Zealots

# Open-Source Agile Publication

In the journey of learning how to write a book, inspired by the Agile Movement and the Open Source community, I come to these principles that will lead the writing of this book:

## 1) Free as in Freedom

The publication, unless otherwise specified, is distributed under the Creative Commons BY-SA[22] license. This gives the freedom to copy, share and show in public this material with any media and create derivate work for any purpose, even commercially, under the following terms:

- **Attribution** — You must give appropriate credit, provide a link to the license, and indicate if changes were made. You may do so in any reasonable manner, but not in any way that suggests the licensor endorses you or your use.
- **ShareAlike** — If you remix, transform, or build upon the material, you must distribute your contributions under the same license as the original.
- **No additional restrictions** — You may not apply legal terms or technological measures that legally restrict others from doing anything the license permits.

---

[22]https://creativecommons.org/licenses/by-sa/3.0/

## 2) On the shoulder of giants

This publication will not reinvent the wheel and will not waste your time expressing in different words somebody else's ideas to avoid plagiarism. When another publication is considered exhaustive on a specific topic will be quoted and linked, leaving the reader the decision if invest time in learning more from the source. Sources available with the same permissive license will be preferred over restricted material.

## 3) Early and Continuous delivery of valuable content

The highest priority is to delight the readers through early and continuous delivery of fresh, valuable content. We will try to do that frequently. We will simplify the new content's navigation with a Hyper Textual Change Log at the beginning of the publication.

## 4) Ultimate Edition

Multiple editions will be published, adding every time new stories and practices discovered with clients. The readers who buy the book from any source will get free access to the electronic version, continually updated on Leanpub[23]. Nobody will need to pay for future editions, and everybody will receive all the updates forever. It's a promise!

Sharing my work with the **Open-Source Agile Publication principles** is the best way I know to create a better world and give thanks to the giants who came before us.

---

[23]https://leanpub.com/scrum-ai/

# How to get the updates

Due to some restrictions following the GDPR law, Leanpub is not automatically subscribing new users to the updates' mailing list. So to be sure to be notified every time there's a new version available (don't worry, it will be one email per month, or less), go on your Leanpub's account, "Library" -> "Books." Then, select the book "Scrum in AI," mark "New Version available" under Email Settings.

How to subscribe to updates notification

# Introducing myself

**As the** Author
**I want** to introduce myself
**So that** the readers know the context from where I learned this book's material.

My name is Paolo Sammicheli, Sammy to my friends. I was born in Siena - Italy, a charming town in Southern Tuscany, famous for its Palio[24], an ancient horse race held twice a year. I am a computer scientist. Technology has always been my passion. I was eleven when I first tried to program a computer. It was my Commodore 64, an absolute novelty for those times and a luxury. It had just arrived from faraway America, and it cost nearly one million Italian Liras, around 500€ today, but given the cost of living at that time was a real asset for a kid like me. We were pioneers in the early eighties: we programmed in BASIC, and software was loaded using 5¼-inch floppy disks or cassette tapes. I soon realized that this was what I wanted to do in my life, and, at nineteen years old, Information Technology became my profession.

I got my diploma in Computer Science from the Industrial School in 1991, and I immediately started working in IT Firms.

As a teenager, I volunteered for many years, driving ambulances for the Misericordia di Siena[25], a 750-year-old welfare organization, and also taking part in humanitarian expeditions in Italy and abroad with the Civil Protection Group. When, in the late 1990s, I discovered the Free Software[26], it was love at first sight. All those programs developed by volunteers, which you could legally

---

[24]https://en.wikipedia.org/wiki/Palio_di_Siena
[25]http://www.misericordiadisiena.it
[26]https://en.wikipedia.org/wiki/Free_software

copy, study and modify, represented a technology plus volunteering combination that I sensed particularly close to my vision of the world. I was one of the most active members in the Siena Linux User Group[27]. My friends were there too, and we organized conferences and events to raise awareness on free software in schools, universities, and sometimes even in town squares.

The free operating system that was spreading most rapidly in the 2000s was Ubuntu[28]. In the Bantu language, spoken in Central Africa, Ubuntu means "humanity towards others" or "I am what I am because of who we all are." Building a better computer system, accessible and free for everybody: this was the vision of the project's founder, the South African entrepreneur Mark Shuttleworth[29]. I joined the project in 2006, and thanks to my volunteering, I quickly earned the Italian community's esteem and friendship. Towards the end of 2007, I mainly dealt with translation and marketing. I founded the **Italian Ubuntu Marketing Team**. I had set the goal of organizing in-person gatherings for the community members who usually had online contacts only.

When, in 2008, I started contributing to the international community and traveling every year to the US to attend the Ubuntu Developer Summit, I was employed by an Italian Software company as the Technical Directory of the central Italy branch.

Thanks to the Ubuntu International community, I first glanced at how an Agile Organization would look. From the technical point of view, the organization was impressive: we had 3000 remote contributors worldwide, developing, testing, and releasing software with automated tests and continuous integration daily. The operating system's stable version had a release cycle of six months, less than one-quarter of any other commercial operative system. From a cultural point of view, the community was an incredibly welcoming and collaborative environment. The morale

---

[27]http://siena.linux.it
[28]https://www.ubuntu.com
[29]https://en.wikipedia.org/wiki/Mark_Shuttleworth

was exceptionally high, and even though there were highly talented people, the ego was usually low. I fell in love with Agility, and I started applying to the company I was employed in, even though the culture was not so welcoming and the results very different. I didn't give up and enrolled in a Certified Scrum Master and a Product Owner class to learn more.

From 2008 I experienced this double professional life, with fun and stellar productivity in Ubuntu and frustration and unproductivity in my daily job. Finally, in 2014, not too fond of my employer's politics, I decided to resign. I started my career change, founding my own company with Alessandro, an ex-colleague that left the company just after me.

My company was supposed to be mainly a Software Firm and offering Agile coaching and training as a complementary business. The same year Agile became very popular in Italy, so client after client, I found myself working as a full-time Agile Business Coach and leaving my company's software development side to Alessandro. To me, that meant moving from Silicon to Carbon, in other words, from working with computers to people.

From 2016 I had the opportunity to implement Scrum with Hardware in an Industrial context. I met Joe Justice, a Scrum Trainer founder of the Wikispeed project[30], and other pioneers in the journey of learning more of the Scrum applied to Hardware development. This experience gave me the incredible opportunity to speak in a TEDx[31] about this topic. Since then, Joe and I became close friends, and I have been lucky enough to co-train with him multiple times in the US and Europe, and visit clients. In 2017 I transformed my diaries of these fantastic experiences with him in my first book: Scrum for Hardware[32]. The fate was nice to me: this book has been recognized as the first significant publication in the world on the topic and received considerable exposition in the US,

---

[30]https://en.wikipedia.org/wiki/Wikispeed
[31]http://scrum-hardware.com/tedxsiena-paolo-sammicheli/
[32]https://leanpub.com/Scrum-for-Hardware

Europe, and Japan.

My book's success led me to meet and co-train with Jeff Suther-land[33], co-author of Scrum, the Agile Manifesto, and founder of Scrum Inc[34]. After some training together, Jeff asked me if I was interested in becoming a licensed trainer for his company. My career took a boost: as a Scrum Inc's Scrum Trainer, I taught and coached Scrum Teams in successful companies in a wide range of industries: Machinery, Construction, Oil&Gas, IoT, Pharmaceutical, Banking, Food, Beverages, Aeronautics, and Aerospace.

In 2019, I got interested in Artificial Intelligence thanks to a random beer with a former GoogleX Engineer who was spending his holidays in Tuscany. The same year, AI's interest increased within my clients, and they started developing Artificial Intelligence applications. From that point, I've been asked multiple times to coach teams developing AI.

In March 2020, during the first Italian lockdown due to the Covid-19 Pandemic, I took advantage of the lonely weekends at home to enroll in an online Artificial Intelligence course at MIT Sloan, where I learned a lot and met incredibly talented people.

I don't consider myself an expert at all on the topic of Artificial Intelligence. You're reading this book because I decided to put in order and publish the notes and the learning I am having in this never-ending journey. This book is written iteratively, following the Agile approach. In this way, I hope to bring the best I know about the subject to the public in the shortest time and receive feedback to create the best book on how to develop an Ai-based application with Agile.

---

[33]https://en.wikipedia.org/wiki/Jeff_Sutherland
[34]https://www.scruminc.com

# Fundamentals

**As the** Author
**I want** to recap the fundamentals
**So that** anybody can enjoy this book regardless of the
level of experience.

## Is this first part for you?

In this part, I'll recap Agility's basic notions, not explicitly related to
AI development. Seasoned Agile practitioners would be tempted to
skip this first part. From a certain point of view, they might be right.
I recommend browsing these chapters anyway, especially the Open
and Inner Source and the Scrum Pattern chapters. I often found this
topics to be unknown to the majority of Agile practitioners. Scrum
Inc. teaches the Scrum Patterns starting from the two-day Scrum
Master class, typically considered the entry-level training. Having
co-trained with Jeff Sutherland multiple times, I feel this material to
be part of the basics. Other Scrum certification bodies and respected
trainers do not teach the Scrum Patterns, and many people consider
them an optional topic or just for seasoned coaches. So, be sure
not to miss it because I'll mention them during the second part,
explicitly covering AI development, without explaining what a
Pattern is.

# Artificial Intelligence

**As the** Author
**I want** to introduce the topic of AI
**So that** I can later start introducing the subject of developing it with Agile and Scrum

## AI Definition and overview

The term Artificial Intelligence can be hard to define. The shortest definition of Artificial Intelligence I know comes from Prof. Thomas Malone[35], the Patrick J. McGovern Professor of Management at the MIT Sloan School of Management and the founding director of the MIT Center for Collective Intelligence:

> "Artificial Intelligence is machine acting in ways that seem intelligent."

Forrester, instead, defines AI as:

> "A system, built through coding, business rules, and increasingly self-learning capabilities, that can supplement human cognition and activities and interacts with humans natural, but also understands the environment, solves human problems, and performs human tasks."

What are the human tasks commonly associated with intelligence?

- Perceiving: Seeing, listening, sensing, etc.

---

[35]https://en.wikipedia.org/wiki/Thomas_W._Malone

- Learning, knowing, reasoning: Thinking, understanding, planning, etc.
- Communicating: Speaking, writing, etc.
- Acting, Reacting, and Interacting.

The different areas of AI can be structured according to those behaviors, like in the following simplified schema from "Applied Artificial Intelligence" by Bernhard G. Humm.[36]

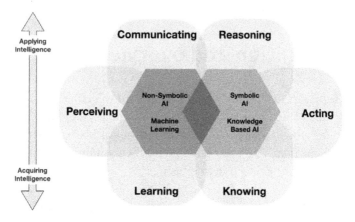

Following the association between the Human Tasks and AI branches:

- Perceiving includes computer vision and sensor technology
- Communicating includes natural language processing
- Learning includes machine learning, information retrieval, and data mining
- Knowing includes knowledge representation
- Reasoning includes logic programming, probabilistic reasoning, and complex event processing
- Acting includes planning, agent technology, and robotics

---

[36]Applied Artificial Intelligence, Bernhard Humm: https://leanpub.com/AAI

The hexagons in the center of the picture show the
Two fundamentally different approaches to AI:

- Symbolic AI, where knowledge is represented explicitly with symbols in a human-readable way
- Non-symbolic AI, where knowledge is implicit in the form of numbers

Artificial Intelligence is the kind of word that MIT's Professor Marvin Minsky[37] defined as "suitcase word": terms where you can stuff anything into. That's the reason that this chapter could become a book itself. So, to keep it short, I will briefly describe the three main types of AI: Machine Learning, Natural Language Processing, and Robotics.

## Machine Learning

Machine learning (ML) is the study of computer algorithms that improve automatically through experience.[38] Machine learning algorithms build a model based on sample data, known as "training data," to make predictions or decisions without being explicitly programmed to do so.[39]

Machine learning can also be defined as the process of solving a practical problem by 1) gathering a dataset and 2) algorithmically building a statistical model based on that dataset. That statistical model is assumed to be used somehow to solve the practical problem.[40]

Machine learning approaches are traditionally divided into four broad categories:

---

[37] https://it.wikipedia.org/wiki/Marvin_Minsky

[38] Mitchell, Tom (1997). Machine Learning. New York: McGraw Hill.

[39] The definition "without being explicitly programmed" is often attributed to Arthur Samuel, who coined the term "machine learning" in 1959

[40] The Hundred-Page Machine Learning Book, Andriy Burkov - What is Machine Learning: https://leanpub.com/theMLbook

- Supervised Learning: The computer is presented with an example of the inputs and labels of the desired outputs, called training data or dataset.
- Semi-Supervised Learning: The computer is presented with a dataset containing both labeled and unlabeled examples. The goal is the same as Supervised Learning. The hope here is that using many unlabeled examples can help the learning algorithm to produce a better model.
- Unsupervised Learning: No training data are given to the learning algorithm, leaving it on its own to find structure in its input. Unsupervised learning can be a goal in itself (discovering hidden patterns in data) or a means towards an end (feature learning).
- Reinforcement Learning: A computer program interacts with a dynamic environment to perform a specific goal. As it navigates its problem space, the program is provided feedback that's analogous to rewards, which it tries to maximize.

Other approaches that do not naturally fit into this three-fold categorization are topic modeling, dimensionality reduction, and meta-learning. Often, the machine learning system features more than one approach.[41]

## Natural Language Processing

Natural language processing (NLP) is the study of interactions between computers and human language. The most common NLP Tasks include recognition of language in written and speech, text and speech generation, Morphological and Syntactic analysis, Lexical and Relational semantics, High-level NLP like text summarization, dialogue management, grammatical correction, translations, and question answering.[42]

---

[41]https://en.wikipedia.org/wiki/Machine_learning#Machine_learning_approaches
[42]https://en.wikipedia.org/wiki/Natural_language_processing

## Robotics

Robotics is an interdisciplinary field that integrates computer science and engineering to design machines that can help humans.

It's a broad field that includes anthropomorphic machinery, animal-like robots, and devices spanning from wheels to flying and driving vehicles.

Software robots (bots) are also considered part of Robotics. Their goal is to mimic a human worker to handle high-volume, repeatable tasks.[43]

# AI as a General Purpose Technology

"General-purpose technologies" (GPTs) are technologies that affect an entire economy (usually at a national or global level). These technologies have the potential to drastically alter societies through their impact on pre-existing economic and social structures. Examples of GPTs include the steam engine, railroad, interchangeable parts, electricity, electronics, mechanization, the automobile, the computer, and the Internet. [44]

Artificial Intelligence is considered one of the more prominent GPTs of the modern era since it possesses the typical three fundamental features or characteristics:

1. It is pervasive and adopted by most sectors.
2. It is inherently developed and improves over time.
3. It catalyzes innovation in complementary technologies, creating new markets, products or processes.

And still, in many companies, I found resistance to try and adopt such technology. This situation reminds me of a story about the advent of the Electric Engine. [45]

---

[43]https://en.wikipedia.org/wiki/Robotics
[44]https://en.wikipedia.org/wiki/General-purpose_technology
[45]https://www.bbc.com/news/business-40673694

When corporations at the end of 1800 invested in electric dynamos and motors installing them in the workplace, the expected surge in productivity did not come. By 1900, less than 5% of mechanical drive power in American factories came from electric motors. The Age of Steam lingered. Why? The original factories built around the steam engine were developed vertically, around the central engine. The early adopter of the Electric Engine used it just as a substitution for the Steam Engine.

They improved the work environment and saved some money, that's true, but without getting the substantial advantage: Electricity could be taken where needed with just a cable. Also, small electric engines were just efficient as big ones, something impossible with steam.

Wiring and small engines allowed the development of horizontal factories, inventing the assembly chain, and increasing productivity by revolutionizing the production process.

But to see this, we needed to wait more than 30 years: the existing management class, coming from the old mindset, didn't recognize this innovation. Only when a new generation of managers went into the companies, we've seen a rapid and radical shift.

# The beauty of AI

My fascination with Artificial Intelligence and Machine Learning comes from different things.
First, it allows solving problems that with traditional software development were impossible to solve.

My interest also comes from the fact that it completely changes the development approach. In conventional software development, you provide the machine the input and the instruction to get the desired output. With AI, you give the conditions to allow the computer to figure out the instructions by itself.

Finally, the beauty is also that the system can keep learning with the experience. It's not static anymore. This automatic continuous improvement may be a great opportunity but also a source of new challenges.

# The Challenges to Developing AI

There are many challenges when developing an AI-Based application that sums up with the traditional software development challenges.

## Black Box Problem

The fact that artificial intelligence algorithms are machine-generated through training creates the problem that humans cannot read and understand. The internal behavior is unknown, and this makes them slightly unreliable. When the algorithm's output is as expected, everything is ok. But incredible frustration comes when the behavior is not as expected. What to do? Several systems are being studied to address this problem. One example is LIME[46] (Local Interpretable Model-Agnostic Explanations). LIME allows you to provide insight into the data that led to an outcome. Therefore, providing an idea of the logic behind the decisions reduces the black box problem, making the algorithm generally more reliable. At the time of writing this paragraph, however, the problem is by no means solved and remains one of the most heartfelt issues facing AI developers.

## Testing

Testing AI appears to be a real challenge. The stable models, those that don't evolve over time through experience, seem easier to

---

[46]https://www.oreilly.com/content/introduction-to-local-interpretable-model-agnostic-explanations-lime/

test. The available data set, hence the annotated data to build the machine learning solution, is divided between the Training Data and the Test Data. With the Test Data not provided to the machine during the training, Developers get an idea about the resulting algorithm's accuracy. This could be re-used for Testing the system again and ensuring that nothing is broken along the time.

A different situation comes when you have an algorithm that evolves over time. An example would be a text summarization function. How can you test if the output with a given input is a plausible summarization? And if this changes, how can you question if this is an improvement or degradation of the algorithm? Today only a human being, an expert of the domain, can be the source of truth to rely on.

## Debugging

Let alone the problem debugging the AI model itself, described above in the Black Box Problem, debugging the neural network code also looks challenging. Examples of nasty bugs can be found in the Article "How to unit test machine learning code[47]" by Chase Roberts. This problem can be mitigated by creating Unit Tests following the Test-Driven Development approach. Even though the author of the article himself found this approach to be rare and «even places like OpenAI only found bugs by staring at every line of their code and try to think why it would cause a bug.»

## Estimates

My observation is that companies that are still anchored to the idea that software development is an industrial process and therefore plannable with annual timescales will come to Agility when developing AI-based applications. AI models do not provide exact

---

[47]https://medium.com/@keeper6928/how-to-unit-test-machine-learning-code-57cf6fd81765

results, like black or white. Let's say you want to train a model to distinguish cats and dogs in a photo. The result will be that a given image is for a probability of 85% a cat and for 15% a dog. Let's assume that the developers needed a terabyte of data and six months of work to get this result. Now, imagine that stakeholders ask, "85% is not enough, how long does it take to get to 90% of confidence?" This answer is impossible to give. Using twice development time and twice data, the accuracy could go up by only one percent or as much as five. And then it could be that one morning a scientific paper comes out with a different technique and, with the same data and a few minutes of tuning, it achieves 95% accuracy. Managers hate this kind of situation, but this is ordinary with a complex development like artificial intelligence.

## Disrupting innovation

With the uncertainty about how long development would take, there's the uncertainty of how long this will last.

With the unseen innovation we're facing, a solution that today looks excellent may become obsolete next month: a new scientific paper gets published, a competitor gets an insight, they evolve their model, and here's that your product needs an update urgently, not to become obsolete. How to cope with quickly emerging requirements like these? How to calculate the ROI? The traditional project funding process will miserably fail in this context without a mindset shift.

## Data Quality

If AI is the new engine of the modern world, then data will be the new energy source. Data quality becomes then dramatically important.

Frequent advice is to build a catalog of assets or a Data Lake[48].

---
[48]https://en.wikipedia.org/wiki/Data_lake

A data catalog allows informed decisions — once you've got a centralized record of assets, you can start to do things like bringing data together and making it searchable.

The question is, with companies producing an exponentially growing set of data, where every single employee individually creates, on a daily basis, hundreds of megabytes, if not more, how could this be achievable? Wouldn't it be like trying to catalog bubbles in a boiling water tank?

The need for AI capable of understanding unordered and unstructured information is becoming more challenging every day but a real need.

In addition to this, high-quality, valuable data to combine with the internal data company have could be expensive to get. And regulations make it even more difficult.

## Data Drift and Concept Drift

A Machine Learning model cannot be considered finished once it has been developed and deployed. Data Drift or Concept Drift may occur at some time.

When **Data Drift** occurs, your model's training data are no longer accurate, typically due to seasonal variations or evolving customer preferences. For instance, before Covid, educational data revealed a lower propensity for online learning than after Covid. Similar to how the demand for face masks increased and the use for lipsticks has significantly decreased.

**Concept Drift**, in contrast to Data Drift, happens when the expected target of the model or its statistical characteristics alter over time. The model learns a function that maps the target variable during training, but with time it loses the ability to use the patterns in a new setting. For instance, in spam detection, models have to be updated since the definition of spam has evolved.

As a result, your production model would be stale at some point for one reason or the other. Therefore, you will need to monitor and retrain your models after release. And your Product Owner needs to explain this to the stakeholders that need to be counted in budgeting consideration before starting.

## The Bias Problem

People worry about bias: stories of AI systems being "prejudiced" against women or minorities make the news headlines repeatedly. But how does that happen? Unquestionably, AI cannot have bad intentions.

The nature of an AI depends on the amount of data it is trained on. So, the ability to use good data is the solution to sound AI systems in the future. In reality, the quality of the data companies collect is poor.

The data sets are biased and only define the nature and specifications of a limited number of people with common interests like religion, gender, ethnicity, etc. Natural evolution can be brought only by defining some algorithms that can efficiently track these kinds of problems.

This happened in Amazon recruitment, where it's being discovered that the AI recruiter was gender-biased. Since most of the technical departments' workforce is men, the system learned that male applicants are preferable and penalized the women's resumes. Multiple examples can be found in Kaja Polachowska's article "Artificial intelligence in review: when AI fails[49]"

The Bias Problem is a big challenge. Gerald Numan, in the chapter "Testing Artificial Intelligence[50]" from the book "The Future of Software Quality Assurance[51]", says:

---

[49]https://neoteric.eu/blog/artificial-intelligence-in-review-when-ai-fails/
[50]https://link.springer.com/chapter/10.1007/978-3-030-29509-7_10
[51]https://link.springer.com/book/10.1007/978-3-030-29509-7

An AI tester needs moral, social, and worldly intelligence and awareness to bring out the users and their expectations and translate them into test cases that can be run repetitively and automated. AI testing includes setting up metrics that translate test results into a meaningful and quantifiable evaluation system for developers to optimize the system.

And there is an important thing we should consider in terms of bias: data comes from people. People lie. People spread stereotypes. Who will control the controller?

## Cybersecurity

The ENISA (European Union Agency for Cybersecurity), the Union's agency established in 2004 and dedicated to achieving a high level of Cybersecurity across Europe, published in December 2020 the report "Artificial Intelligence Cybersecurity Challenges[52]." In this very detailed report they included:

- The definition of the scope of AI in the context of Cybersecurity, following a lifecycle approach from requirements analysis to deployment.
- The Identification of assets of the AI ecosystem to clarify what needs to be protected and what could go wrong.
- The mapping of the AI threats with a detailed taxonomy.
- The classification of threats for the different assets and in the context of the diverse AI lifecycle stages, also listing relevant threat actors.

The list of threats, presented at a high level and then detailed accurately, is impressive. They listed:

---

[52]https://www.enisa.europa.eu/publications/artificial-intelligence-cybersecurity-challenges

- Nefarious activity/abuse (NAA): "intended actions that target ICT systems, infrastructure, and networks by means of malicious acts with the aim to either steal, alter, or destroy a specified target."
- Eavesdropping/Interception/ Hijacking (EIH): "actions aiming to listen, interrupt, or seize control of a third party communication without consent."
- Physical attacks (PA): "actions which aim to destroy, expose, alter, disable, steal or gain unauthorised access to physical assets such as infrastructure, hardware, or interconnection."
- Unintentional Damage (UD): unintentional actions causing "destruction, harm, or injury of property or persons and results in a failure or reduction in usefulness."
- Failures or malfunctions (FM): "Partial or full insufficient functioning of an asset (hardware or software)."
- Outages (OUT): "unexpected disruptions of service or decrease in quality falling below a required level. "
- Disaster (DIS): "a sudden accident or a natural catastrophe that causes great damage or loss of life."
- Legal (LEG): "legal actions of third parties (contracting or otherwise), in order to prohibit actions or compensate for loss based on applicable law."

«Protecting AI models and the AI development environment may soon be the Chief Security Officer's greatest challenge, given the complexity of the underlying big data platforms and the mathematics required to understand many of the esoteric—yet very real—attacks against modern AI algorithms.» wrote Gene Geddes and Chris Konrad in the article "An Introduction to AI Model Security[53]." How to cope with this? Nicola Vanin[54], AI Domain expert at Cedacri Spa and ION Group CISO, posted on Linkedin[55] what I think is the essence of this topic:

---

[53]https://www.wwt.com/article/introduction-to-ai-model-security
[54]https://www.linkedin.com/in/nicola-vanin-b03a5451/
[55]https://www.linkedin.com/posts/nicola-vanin-b03a5451_sicurezza-software-hardware-activity-6817034549957062656-he37

«Cybersecurity is often addressed only after the software or hardware product is fully developed. The result is disastrous (databreach, bugs, cyberattacks). Therefore, those doing Cybersecurity have an obligation to continually evolve, adapt, and implement quickly to mitigate risks. In my learning journey, it became critical to build an Agile environment, where development teams have the opportunity to integrate security more seamlessly and then identify issues early in the development process, when they are less expensive and time consuming to address. Because Cybersecurity is a journey, not an end state.»

## Regulation

Finally, to increase the risks and complexity of AI development, governments and social movements are reasonably worried about the ethical implication of AI and its impact on society. At the moment of writing, AI gets constant exposition on the news. Just a few weeks ago EU proposed strict AI rules, with fines of up to 6% for violations.[56]

It is clear that the need for continuous adaptation through development is critical in a context like this.

# Further readings

- Artificial Intelligence A Modern Approach[57], Stuart Russell, Peter Norvig
- The Emotion Machine[58], Marvin Minsky

---

[56]https://venturebeat.com/2021/04/21/eu-proposes-strict-ai-rules-with-fines-up-to-6-for-violations/
[57]https://www.goodreads.com/book/show/58023298-artificial-intelligence
[58]https://www.goodreads.com/book/show/169007.The_Emotion_Machine

- Applied Artificial Intelligence[59], Bernhard Humm
- The Hundred-Page Machine Learning Book[60], Andriy Burkov
- Artificial Intelligence Cybersecurity Challenges[61], European Union Agency for Cybersecurity

---

[59]https://leanpub.com/AAI
[60]https://leanpub.com/theMLbook
[61]https://www.enisa.europa.eu/publications/artificial-intelligence-cybersecurity-challenges

# Agile

**As the** Author
**I want** to introduce the topic of Agile
**So that** the reader can understand the real meaning of
Agile without the hype associated with it.

What means Agile? The commonly used definition comes from the
**Agile Manifesto**, described later in this chapter:

Responding to Change over Following a Plan

Nevertheless, before showing the 2001 Agile Manifesto, I would like
to start talking about the more recent definition of Agile I know,
from Alistair Cockburn[62]:

> "Agile is the ability to move and change direction,
> quickly and with ease."

## The Heart of Agile

Alistair Cockburn is one of the 17th authors of the **Agile Manifesto**,
and he recently published "The Heart of Agile[63]."

---

[62]https://en.wikipedia.org/wiki/Alistair_Cockburn
[63]https://heartofagile.com

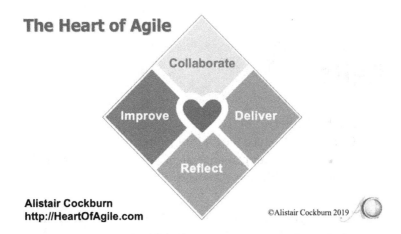

His idea of agility has been synthesized in 4 words: Collaborate, Deliver, Reflect, Improve. The logo itself is a visual tool that allows people to reflect and brainstorm about what these words mean in our context. Alistair provides for each one of the four keywords a set of concepts and tools. By expanding the concept from the center to the exterior, tools can become broader and extensive.

### The Heart expands into Details

# Deliver

## Internal flow

Any organization in the world could be described as a giant brain where there are people making decisions. Everything delivered is an embodiment of decisions, and findings build upon other choices. This internal flow of decisions needs to be visualized and improved to make the organization improve.

From this point of view, anything we deliver is made of Decisions. Alistair's researches show that in every 5-10 decisions, an error is made. How to deal with this then? Alistair says that by making decisions visible with visual management tools, we can improve this flow of decisions with the same principles of Lean Manufacturing[64]. With these practices, we can remove waste and optimizing the flow.

## Deliver for learning

Whenever an organization delivers something, feedback happens. Agility use feedback to build a loop that leads to an improvement constantly. The slight improvement, known as Kaizen in the Japanese tradition, allows for systemic advancement thanks to the constancy. Agile methods like Scrum allow significant changes thanks to frequent replan, in Japanese known as "Kaikaku." Combining intelligently "Kaizen" and "Kaikaku" leads to getting ahead of the competition in organizational learning and getting a competitive advantage.

## Deliver for income

Delivery is always associated with an exchange of value. Frequent deliveries produce a regular return on investments. The reduction of the ROI timing reduces risks and enables the company to provide greater agility.

---

[64]https://en.wikipedia.org/wiki/Lean_manufacturing

# Reflect

## Examine data

This topic includes the behavioral aspects of stopping and inspecting the data and the good habits of collecting and rationalizing data to get insight. Effective use of AI consists of these needs, combined with the big data technologies needed to manage an exponentially growing set of information.

## Introspect

To stop and check data include also checking emotions. We're human beings, and we can only perform if we're comfortable with ourselves. To explore this topic, I suggest looking for the literacy about Retrospectives, especially the book Agile Retrospectives[65] by Diana Larsen and Ester Derby.

# Improve

## Change

In his training, Alistair suggests "Solution Focus" as an approach for this manner. What is Solution Focus? The solution-focused brief therapy approach[66] grew from the work of American social workers Steve de Shazer[67], Insoo Kim Berg[68], and their team at the Milwaukee Brief Family Therapy Center (BFTC) in Milwaukee, Wisconsin.

I found a good description of it in the coachingleaders.co.uk[69] website:

---

[65]https://www.goodreads.com/book/show/721338.Agile_Retrospectives
[66]https://en.wikipedia.org/wiki/Solution-focused_brief_therapy
[67]https://en.wikipedia.org/wiki/Steve_de_Shazer
[68]https://en.wikipedia.org/wiki/Insoo_Kim_Berg
[69]https://coachingleaders.co.uk/what-is-solution-focus/

Solution Focus is a big idea that focuses on small steps and keeping them simple. This means that you can start using it to improve your business and your life straight away. (...) Although it originated as a therapy model, the Solution Focused approach is now being applied to coaching and team and organizational change with great success.

Solution Focus is based on 4 Principles:

- Focus on solutions, not problems
- People already have the resources they need to change
- Change happens in small steps
- Work at the surface level

Even though it is possible to read books to understand the method attending a workshop would be advised. With an in-person seminar, it would be easier to learn how to use the technique with individuals and teams.

### Experiment

Every time you will improve something, that is because you change it. But not every change will be an improvement. So, the best way is to proceed with changing stuff with small experiments. For this topic, I personally recommend PopcornFlow, by Claudio Perrone. It's a system of continuous experimentation that I found very useful, especially in complex problems. You can find more information about it in the Appendix, where I interviewed the author.

## Collaborate

### Collaboration and Communication

The ability to communicate and collaborate effectively is vital to have a functional work environment. Alistair, in his workshop, teaches multiple techniques to improve collaboration, primarily based on visualization and enabling everybody to express themselves.

## Culture and Trust

A team is not a group of people working together. It's a group of people who trust each other[70].
Culture could be defined as a set of Values and Beliefs shared in an organization. Although it is being cultivated or not, organizational culture exists and drives the decisions not regulated, made in a discretional way. Often only 20% of the decisions at work are driven by specific rules and norms. 80% of the decisions are driven by values and a set of shared beliefs. Cultivating the Company Culture is vital if we want most of the findings to align with the organization's strategy.

An excellent example of how an organization can develop and nurture its culture is the Zappos case study. I highly recommend the book Delivering Happiness[71] by the late Tony Hsieh[72], an easy to read and incredibly inspiring book, also available as an audiobook read by the author.

# The Agile Manifesto

The original Agile Manifesto[73] has been created during a meeting in 2001 at Snowbird Utah.
The 17 participants came from different backgrounds and methods: eXtreme Programming, Scrum, DSDM, and other software consultants. They come out with a set of shared values that considered the essence of all the methods represented.

---

[70]Quote by Simon Sinek: https://www.osmquote.com/quote/simon-sinek-quote-5b40d4
[71]https://en.wikipedia.org/wiki/Delivering_Happiness
[72]https://en.wikipedia.org/wiki/Tony_Hsieh
[73]https://agilemanifesto.org

# Manifesto for Agile Software Development

We are uncovering better ways of developing
software by doing it and helping others do it.
Through this work we have come to value:

**Individuals and interactions** over **processes and tools**

**Working software** over **comprehensive documentation**

**Customer collaboration** over **contract negotiation**

**Responding to change** over **following a plan**

That is, while there is value in the items on
the right, we value the items on the left more.

# Principles behind the Agile Manifesto

After the meeting, the participants kept talking through emails about what the Manifesto meant, in practice, and published twelve principles behind it:

1. Our highest priority is to satisfy the customer through early and continuous delivery of valuable software.
2. Welcome changing requirements, even late in development. Agile processes harness change for the customer's competitive advantage.
3. Deliver working software frequently, from a couple of weeks to a couple of months, with a preference to the shorter timescale.
4. Business people and developers must work together daily throughout the project.
5. Build projects around motivated individuals. Give them the environment and support they need, and trust them to get the job done.

6. The most efficient and effective method of conveying information to and within a development team is face-to-face conversation.
7. Working software is the primary measure of progress.
8. Agile processes promote sustainable development. The sponsors, developers, and users should be able to maintain a constant pace indefinitely.
9. Continuous attention to technical excellence and good design enhances agility.
10. Simplicity–the art of maximizing the amount of work not done–is essential.
11. The best architectures, requirements, and designs emerge from self-organizing teams.
12. At regular intervals, the team reflects on how to become more effective, then tunes and adjusts its behavior accordingly.

# Today: Product, not Software

After the Manifesto publishing, some authors pointed out that the Manifesto wasn't really about software only but could be applied to any product. There wasn't a general consensus about rephrasing it for a more general purpose, so it remained unchanged from the first formulation. However, many Agile Manifesto authors, I have seen Jeff Sutherland and Alistair Cockburn, override the word "software" with "product" in their presentations and course material to make the Agile Manifesto usable in a more general way.

# Further readings

- Agile Software Development[74] - Alistair Cockburn

---

[74]https://www.goodreads.com/book/show/942577.Agile_Software_Development

- Agile and Iterative Development: A Manager's Guide[75] - Craig Larman
- The Age of Agile[76] - Steve Denning

---

[75]https://www.goodreads.com/book/show/1229810.Agile_and_Iterative_Development
[76]https://www.goodreads.com/book/show/34963438-the-age-of-agile

# Scrum

**As the** Author
**I want** to introduce the topic of Scrum
**So that** I clarify what is Scrum and what is not

In some way, Machine Learning in computers reminds me of how Scrum works with teams and organizations compared to traditional methodologies. With a process framework like Scrum, you don't provide a detailed description of the structure and the expected processes and behavior. Instead, you create a feedback loop and the time to reflect and adapt, and magically the organization evolves, reprogramming itself. So let's take a look at how Scrum works.

## Scrum Basics

**Scrum** is an Agile framework designed to develop complex projects, created by Jeff Sutherland and Ken Schwaber and presented for the first time at the OOPSLA 1995 Conference[77]. Scrum and its rules are described in the Scrum Guide[78], freely available online. However, the best definition of Scrum comes from the recent update of the Scrum Guide, November 2020:

> Scrum is a lightweight framework that helps people, teams, and organizations generate value through adaptive solutions for complex problems.

> In a nutshell, Scrum requires a Scrum Master to foster an environment where:

---

[77]http://www.jeffsutherland.org/oopsla/schwapub.pdf
[78]https://scrumguides.org

- A Product Owner orders the work for a complex problem into a Product Backlog.
- The Scrum Team turns a selection of the work into an Increment of value during a Sprint.
- The Scrum Team and its stakeholders inspect the results and adjust for the next Sprint.
- Repeat

The Scrum Framework elements are eleven: **3 Roles, 5 Events, and 3 Artifacts**. According to the authors, any implementation lacking even just one of these cannot be called Scrum since they are meant to reinforce each other.

The 3 **Roles** of Scrum, described as "Accountabilities," are *Scrum Master, Product Owner,* and *Developers.* Collectively they are called the **Scrum Team**.

The Scrum Master is accountable for establishing Scrum as defined in the Scrum Guide. They do this by helping everyone understand Scrum theory and practice, both within the Scrum Team and the organization. In addition, the Scrum Master is accountable for the Scrum Team's effectiveness. They do this by enabling the Scrum Team to improve its practices within the Scrum framework. In other terms, Scrum Master's accountability is to improve the productivity of the Scrum Team.

The Product Owner is accountable for maximizing the value resulting from the Scrum Team's work. The Product Owner is also accountable for effective Product Backlog management, like creating and clearly communicating Product Backlog Items, managing stakeholders' expectations and defining Product Backlog items' priority. The Product Owner may do the mentioned activities or may delegate the responsibility to others. Regardless, the Product Owner remains accountable.

Developers are the Scrum Team professionals committed to creating any aspect of a usable Increment for each Sprint.

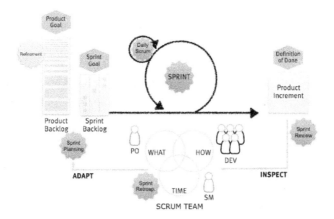

Scrum's artifacts, *Product Backlog, Sprint Backlog,* and the *Increment,* represent work or value. They are designed to maximize the transparency of essential information.

Each artifact contains a commitment to ensure it provides information that enhances transparency and focus so that they can measure the progress:

- For the Product Backlog, it is the Product Goal.
- For the Sprint Backlog, it is the Sprint Goal.
- For the Increment, it is the Definition of Done.

These commitments exist to reinforce empiricism and the Scrum values for the Scrum Team and their stakeholders.

The Product Backlog is a list of *items* sorted by value containing the product's information to be developed. The Product Owner is solely responsible for its prioritization.

The Sprint Backlog is a list of *items* that have to be developed during the Sprint.

An Increment is a concrete step ahead toward the Product Goal. Each Increment consist of the done work performed during the

Sprint integrated with the Increments produced in the previous Sprints. To provide value, the Increment must be usable, hence compliant to the Definition of Done.

The Scrum Team works in iterations of constant duration, called Sprint; every Sprint has a maximum length of 4 weeks and acts as a container for all Scrum events. During the Sprint, the following *events* take place:

- *Sprint Planning* is the meeting at the beginning of the Sprint that lays out the work to be performed for the Sprint. This resulting plan is created by the collaborative work of the entire Scrum Team.
- *Daily Meeting* takes place every day, for no more than 15 minutes, in the same place and at the same time. During the Daily, the Developers align on the previous day's work, the work to be carried out the same day, and possible difficulties.
- *Sprint Review*, a meeting at the end of the Sprint, open to the Scrum Team and any concerned stakeholders to inspect the work produced during the Sprint to determine future adaptations.
- *Retrospective*, a meeting that takes place immediately after the Review and concluding the Sprint. The Scrum Team considers any improvements and organizes accordingly.

Finally, the *Product Backlog Refinement* is the continuous activity where the Scrum Team creates, detail, clarify and estimates the Product Backlog Items for the future Sprints.

## A Healthy Tension

The reason why it is appropriate that three different people embody the three Scrum roles is clearly explained in the video by Henrik Kniberg "PO in a NUTSHELL[79]". In developing a product of any type, there are three objectives we want to achieve.

---

[79]https://www.youtube.com/watch?v=502ILHjX9EE

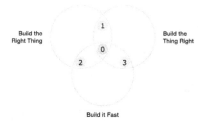

- *Build the right thing*: we want to build the right and valuable product functionality for our clients.
- *Build the thing right*: we want to build the right product from an engineering perspective.
- *Build it fast*: we want to get to the market as quickly as possible.

Ideally, everyone wants to be at point **0** of the diagram, perfectly balanced between the three elements. What happens if we find ourselves at point **1**? We built the right product, and we did it technically very well. However, we have been too slow, and our competitors have already conquered the best customers. The road is uphill, and we will hardly manage to make up for a lost time.

What happens if we find ourselves at point **2** instead? We built the right product quickly. However, our product is technically fragile, customers complain, and medium-term correction of defects and maintenance costs kill the company's profits. Certainly not a good deal. Finally, what happens if we find ourselves at point **3**? We built a beautiful cathedral in record time. Unfortunately, our clients did not want a cathedral — they just wanted a tent. So our expensive product will remain on the shelves gathering dust. Scrum's organization seeks to keep the projects close to point **0** by dividing prerogatives between the three roles.

The *Product Owner* will focus primarily on understanding what features are beneficial and more valuable; that is, "*the right thing*."
The *Developers* will focus on building the product in a technically effective way or building "*the thing right*."

The *Scrum Master* will focus on the process, so productivity increases and reduces the feedback loop.

The faster the learning cycle, the more the Scrum Team will understand how to maintain stability near point **0**. This *Healthy Tension* is the reason for having these three distinct accountabilities.

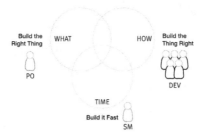

# Develop competencies

Scrum requires the Scrum Team to be cross-functional. All the skills necessary to create the product reside in the team to carry out all the processing steps during the Sprint. It may be that people with specialized skills, employed in a non-continuous way during the development cycle, are under-utilized in some phases of the Sprint. To prevent this from happening and allow team self-organization, Scrum encourages the development of T-Shaped Skills in all team members. In this case, the T represents a competence matrix in which each team member has a rudimental skill in each area required by product development. At the same time, he has an advanced level of knowledge in one of the sectors.

What does it mean? Suppose we represent the various skills on a matrix. Junior implies that the person can do some developments under the guidance and the advice of a Master of that skill. Senior means that the person can develop in autonomy, and Master means the person has a deep knowledge of the topic and can teach and mentor Junior people.

In that case, we can see a T-shaped diagram, where each basic skill is placed in a corresponding area involving the product. A piece of Mastery is placed in one of them.

|        | Skill 1 | Skill 2 | Skill 3 | Skill 4 | Skill 5 |   |
|--------|---------|---------|---------|---------|---------|---|
| Junior |         |         |         |         |         |   |
| Senior |         |         |         |         |         |   |
| Master |         |         |         |         |         |   |
|        |         |         |         |         |         |   |

T-Shaped Skills

However, in LeSS - Large Scale Scrum, Craig Larman asserts that to obtain high-performing teams, it is necessary to create the conditions for people to develop pi-shaped skills, i.e., in the form of $\pi$ (pi). Pi Skill means a solid primary skill, a secondary discrete skill, and rudimental skill in all other aspects.

|        | Skill 1 | Skill 2 | Skill 3 | Skill 4 | Skill 5 |   |
|--------|---------|---------|---------|---------|---------|---|
| Junior |         |         |         |         |         |   |
| Senior |         |         |         |         |         |   |
| Master |         |         |         |         |         |   |
|        |         |         |         |         |         |   |

Pi-Shaped Skills

Larman also asserts that, in this situation, people should act as mentors in their primary skill and carry out most of the activities in the secondary skill to continue to deepen the lesser-known subject.

# A Theory of Scrum Team Effectiveness

In June 2021, Jeff Sutherland sent to us the Scrum Trainers licensed by his company, a recent paper from Cornell University by the title "A Theory of Scrum Team Effectiveness[80]" by Christiaan Verwijs and Daniel Russo. This paper, published after a seven-year-long investigation on almost 1.200 Scrum teams, proposed and validated a theory for effective Scrum teams, focussing on the internal dynamics, a topic that is rarely covered in similar researches. Moreover, it results in a formalization of clear recommendations for how organizations can better support Scrum teams.

What does means Team Effectiveness? Two main variables characterized the effectiveness of Scrum teams according to the interviewed teams:

- Stakeholder Satisfaction
- Team Morale

The findings suggest that the most effective Scrum Teams can **release frequently** (in the schema Responsiveness) and have a clear understanding of what their **stakeholders need** (Stakeholders Concern), but not one or the other. Following the picture of the theoretical model.

---

[80]https://arxiv.org/abs/2105.12439

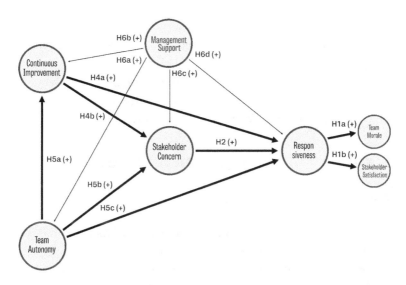

Other factors influence "Stakeholder Concern" and "Responsiveness," and those are being clusterized in Team Autonomy, Continuous Improvement, and Management Support. Then they used the findings from the case studies and insights from extant literature to induce a theoretical model to explain how team-level factors contribute to the effectiveness of Scrum teams and formulated some hypothesis:

- Hypothesis 1 (H1). The Responsiveness of a team is positively associated with team morale (H1a) and stakeholder satisfaction (H1b).
- Hypothesis 2 (H2). Stakeholder concern is positively associated with Responsiveness
- Hypothesis 3 (H3). The positive relationship between stakeholder concern on the one hand, and team morale and stakeholder satisfaction on the other is fully mediated by Responsiveness
- Hypothesis 4 (H4). Continuous improvement is positively associated with stakeholder concern (H4a) and Responsiveness (H4b)

- Hypothesis 5 (H5). Team autonomy is positively associated with continuous improvement (H5a), stakeholder concern (H5b), and Responsiveness (H5c)
- Hypothesis 6 (H6). Management Support is positively associated with team autonomy (H6a), continuous improvement (H6b), stakeholder concern (H6c), and Responsiveness (H6d).

# Summary of Findings and Implications

## Five Factors Team Theory

From 13 case studies, they developed a theoretical model for Scrum teams from thirteen lower-order indicators grouped into five latent factors. This model fits the data from a large and representative sample of Scrum teams well. Furthermore, the five factors explain a substantial amount of variance in stakeholder satisfaction and team morale. As an implication, the suggestion is to design and assess Scrum teams with five team-level factors in mind: Responsiveness, stakeholder concern, continuous improvement, team autonomy, and management support. Then, create the environment of Scrum teams to minimize constraints to these factors on the one hand and train and support them in the skills they need.

## Responsiveness

Responsiveness is positively associated with team morale and stakeholder satisfaction. The suggestion is to support Scrum teams in their ability to be responsive. Implement technical tooling, increase automation, and train necessary skills (particularly the Product Backlog Refinement). Invest in team autonomy, stakeholder concern, and management support to make the need for Responsiveness more relevant to teams.

## Stakeholder Concern

The stakeholder concern of teams is positively associated with Responsiveness. Indirectly, stakeholder concern is also positively associated with Team Morale and stakeholder satisfaction. Nevertheless, this positive effect is only present when Responsiveness is high, i.e., fully mediated by Responsiveness. Product Owners can increase Stakeholder Concern by co-opting teams in product strategy formulation, goal setting, and collaboration with stakeholders. If Scrum teams are unable to release frequently in the first place, efforts must be undertaken to remove organizational constraints, increase automation and build technical skills.

## Continuous Improvement

The degree to which teams engage in continuous improvement is positively associated with stakeholder concern. Contrary to our expectations, continuous improvement is not significantly associated with Responsiveness. Scrum teams are advised to direct their continuous improvement process towards the five critical factors identified in this study: Responsiveness, stakeholder concern, team autonomy, management support, and continuous improvement. These factors are most likely to highlight constraints to team effectiveness stemming from internal or external factors to the team. In turn, organizations should broaden the autonomy of teams to encourage them to take control over improvements.

## Team Autonomy

Team Autonomy was positively associated with continuous improvement and stakeholder concern. Therefore, the recommendation is to expand the autonomy of Scrum Teams primarily in two areas. The first is internal to teams and concerns the degree to which its members are cross-functional. The second concerns constraints imposed by the organizational environment that limit control over tooling, team composition, choice of process, and Product Owners' mandate over their product.

## Management Support

Management Support was found to be positively associated with team autonomy, continuous improvement, and stakeholder concern, but no significant effect was found on Responsiveness. Management can most effectively contribute to Scrum teams by increasing their autonomy, both in self-management and product mandate. Train management in the skills needed to support rather than direct.

# Areas of the Factors

Each factor described in the Theoretical Model, except the Management Factor, are exploded in primary areas:

- Stakeholder Concern
    - Value Focus
    - Stakeholder collaboration
    - Sprint Review Quality
    - Shared Goals
- Team Autonomy
    - Self-Management
    - Cross Functionality
- Continuous Improvement
    - Sprint Retrospective Quality
    - Quality Concern
    - Psychological Safety
    - Shared Learning
- Responsiveness
    - Release Frequency
    - Refinement

The relationship between them and the associated data are depicted in the following picture.

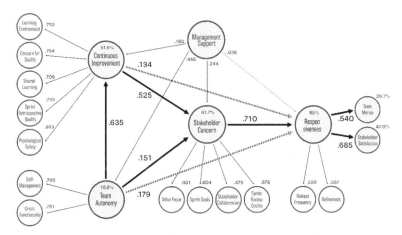

Standardized factor loadings and standardized path coefficients for the research model. All paths, except dotted lines, are significant.

# Further readings

- Scrum: The Art of Doing Twice the Work in Half the Time[81] - Jeff Sutherland
- The Scrum Fieldbook: A Master Class on Accelerating Performance, Getting Results, and Defining the Future[82] - JJ Sutherland
- Software in 30 Days: How Agile Managers Beat the Odds, Delight Their Customers, And Leave Competitors In the Dust[83] - Jeff Sutherland, Ken Schwaber
- A Theory of Scrum Team Effectiveness[84] - Christiaan Verwijs and Daniel Russo

---

[81]https://www.goodreads.com/book/show/19288230-scrum
[82]https://www.goodreads.com/book/show/43582738-the-scrum-fieldbook
[83]https://www.goodreads.com/book/show/13589272-software-in-30-days
[84]https://arxiv.org/abs/2105.12439

# Scrum Patterns

As the Author
I want to introduce the topic of the Scrum Patterns
So that the reader understands how to make high-performing teams and to design effective organizations.

## Scrum Patterns

In software engineering, the concept of *design pattern* can be defined as "a general design solution to a recurring problem." It is a description, or a logical model, applied for resolving a problem that may frequently occur, even before defining the computational part's solving algorithm. It is often a practical approach to contain or reduce technical debt.[85]

Patterns' concept came from Architecture and originated by Christopher Alexander[86], a widely influential British-American architect and design theorist currently emeritus professor at the University of California, Berkeley. His theories about the nature of human-centered design have affected fields beyond architecture, including urban design, software, sociology, and others.

In the late Nineties, The Pattern Language became popular in the Software community. The first Scrum patterns were published in 1997 in a Paper by Mike Beedle, together with Devos, Sharon, Schwaber, and Sutherland with the title SCRUM: An extension pattern language for hyperproductive software development[87]. The

---

[85]Adaptation of the definition of a Design Pattern from Wikipedia: https://en.wikipedia.org/wiki/Design_pattern

[86]https://en.wikipedia.org/wiki/Christopher_Alexander

[87]http://jeffsutherland.org/scrum/scrum_plop.pdf

first Agile Patterns book "Organizational Patterns of Agile Software Development[88]" was published in 2005 by Jim Coplien and Neil Harrison.

Since 2010 the ScrumPlop[89] community meets annually to collect, catalog, and publish the patterns that performing teams around the world adopt using Scrum.

## ScrumPloP Nyteboda, Sweden. 16-19 May 2010

Neil Harrison, Mike Beedle, Jim Coplien, Jeff Sutherland

In 2019, thanks to the work of the ScrumPlop community facilitated by Jim Coplien, who served as a Product Owner, a second book has been published, with the title "A Scrum Book: The Spirit of the Game[90]" by Jim Coplien, Jeff Sutherland and the Scrum Plop community.

# How to Read a Pattern

The structure of a Pattern is meant to simplify the browsing of the publication. Rarely the Patterns books are intended to be read from cover to cover. More frequently are used by reference when in need of a specific source of inspiration. Following a schema of a Pattern's structure.

---

[88]https://www.goodreads.com/book/show/756250.Organizational_Patterns_of_Agile_ Software_Development
[89]http://www.scrumplop.org
[90]https://www.goodreads.com/book/show/45029885-a-scrum-book

# Structure of a Pattern

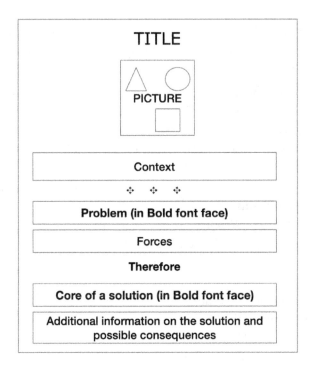

The pattern always has a title and a picture associated. This serves as a way to enable visual memory. Then there's a description of the context and the reference of dependencies from other Patterns. The typographic symbol separates the context from the **Problem** statement in bold font face. Further information of the forces that this problem creates follows, and then the word **Therefore** leads to the core of the **Solution**, still in bold. Underneath the core of the solution, there is detailed information, with examples, images, possible consequences, and a list of sources.

# Teams that Finish Early Accelerate Faster

In 2013 Jeff Sutherland presented at Agile Alliance 2013 in Nashville[91] a talk about nine of what he consider the most useful Scrum Patterns.

He proposed this collection as the first fundamental elements to create a High Performing Team. It's the Scrum Inc. recommended starting point for a Scrum Master, just after implementing the Scrum Guide elements properly. The list of the patterns is the following:

- Stable Teams
- Yesterday's Weather
- Swarming: One-Piece Continuous Flow
- Interrupt Pattern: Illegitimus Non-Interruptus
- Daily Clean Code
- Emergency Procedure
- Scrumming the Scrum
- Happiness Metric
- Teams that Finish Early Accelerate Faster

While the Scrum Guide[92] provides basic Scrum rules, patterns amplify it by showing how teams can solve problems in particular contexts. According to the Scrum authors, Scrum should be simple, fast, and fun. For many new Scrum Masters, Scrum is difficult, slow, and painful instead. Performance patterns are designed to remedy the various headaches encountered by the Scrum Masters in coaching teams' activity.

---

[91]https://www.agilealliance.org/resources/sessions/coaching-simple-patterns-that-avoid-common-pitfalls-for-scrum-teams/

[92]http://scrumguides.org

## Stable Teams

This pattern suggests keeping the teams stable, avoiding moving people continuously from one Team to another. Stable Teams tend to agree and learn more about their skills, making estimates more reliable and allowing the business to be predictable. In traditional organizations, workgroups often change when the project changes; in Agile organizations, the work flows towards stable teams, not vice versa.

## Yesterday's Weather

In many cases, the amount of Product Backlog Items completed during the previous Sprint is the best indicator of the amount of PBIs completed in the following Sprint. With this pattern, the Team plans Sprint items based on the last three sprints' average. When the Team achieves everything before the end of the Sprint, another ready Product Backlog Item will be *pulled* from the Product Backlog in agreement with the PO.

## Swarming: One-Piece Continuous Flow

When a team is struggling to complete the Sprint work, the cause may be that too many things started simultaneously (*work in progress*). This happens if the Team is not focused on finishing first the most valuable item. *Swarming* together on one thing to complete it quickly increases the performance of the entire Sprint. How does it work? Whoever takes charge of the highest priority item is considered the "captain" of the Team. Everyone has to help him, and nobody should interrupt him. As soon as the captain finishes the first item, anyone taking the following item is the new captain.

# Interrupt Pattern: Illegitimus Non-Interruptus

This pattern allows the allocation of a time buffer for any unplanned work and prevents it from exceeding. It is based on three simple rules that will enable the company to organize itself to avoid losing the production rhythm:

1. The Team creates a buffer for interruptions based on historical data. For example, if it turns out that 30% of a team's work comes from unplanned work, with a velocity of 60 points, 20 are reserved for the interruption buffer.
2. All requests must go through the Product Owner. It will be considered whether to insert them in the Product Backlog to do them in the following sprints, reject them entirely, or insert them into the current Sprint interruption buffer. The Team starts working on the new activity only after completing the current one.
3. If the buffer exceeds the maximum size, the Product Owner calls the "Sprint Abort" procedure and notifies the management that release dates may slip.

This last rule means that the buffer does not exceed except in extreme circumstances. If used in conjunction with Yesterday's Weather pattern, its size gradually levels to the minimum possible. A reducing buffer increases the Sprint capacity accordingly and allows the Team to accelerate.

# Daily Clean Code

The correction of problems by the same day they have detected aims to get a flawless project and reduce maintenance costs. It is already known in Lean practices that immediate correction of root problems improves production capacity.

## Emergency Procedure

When the burn-down chart does not show progress towards the Sprint Goal, we suggest this procedure. It is similar to the one used for a long time by the pilots of airplanes.

When a problem emerges, immediately execute the specific emergency procedure without understanding what does not work. It is the responsibility of the Scrum Master to ensure that the procedure is carried out directly, preferably within half of the Sprint. Here are some steps of the emergency procedure. Use the necessary ones:

1. Change the way the work is done. Do something differently.
2. Ask for help, usually by transferring some of the work to someone else.
3. Reduce the Sprint scope.
4. Abort the Sprint and plan again.
5. Inform the management of any impact on the release dates.

## Scrumming the Scrum

Identify the single most crucial impediment and remove it within the next Sprint. The impediment removal item is placed in the Sprint Backlog as a higher priority user story. It is provided with acceptance criteria that determine when it is completed. Then evaluate the state of the story during the Sprint Review along with the others. This pattern was part of the Sprint Retrospective description in the 2017 version of the Scrum Guide[93] and removed again in the 2020 version to simplify the framework.

---

[93] http://scrumguides.org

Sprint Backlog: Day X

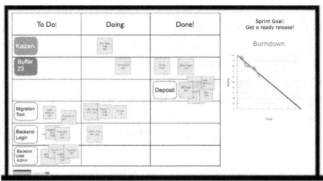

Scrum Board example, by ScrumInc

## Happiness Metric

Happiness is one of the best metrics because it is a predictive indicator. When people think about how happy they are, they are projecting how they feel in the future. If they believe that the company is in trouble or doing something wrong, they will feel sad. If there are any impediments or a frustrating rule system, they will feel sad. A compelling way to understand the status of a team is to know how happy they are. The Scrum Master asks two questions:

- How happy are you about the company?
- How happy are you about your role?

Team members answer questions on a scale of 1 to 5. These numbers are kept in a spreadsheet and tracked weekly. If the numbers change significantly, it is essential to talk with the Team to find ways to make them happier. By monitoring the Team's morale, the Scrum Master successfully anticipates the drops in velocity and acts proactively.

## Teams that Finish Early Accelerate Faster

Teams often accept an excessive workload in the Sprint and cannot finish it. Recognizing failure and being always under pressure are elements that prevent the Team from improving. Therefore, it is advisable to take less work, maximizing the chances of success, using, for example, the Yesterday's Weather pattern. Then, the other Patterns of the list that reduce the Sprint impediments must be implemented, allowing for managing the interruptions and finishing the Sprint Backlog in advance. When the Developers complete the work in advance, it can take the most valuable item from the backlog. This will ensure that the value of Yesterday's Weather grows in the following sprints. To increase the probability of accelerating, it is good to apply Scrumming the Scrum to identify the retrospective's improvement activities and place it as the top priority in the next Sprint.

# Further readings

- ScrumPlop[94] Website
- A Scrum Book[95] - free online version
- A Scrum Book: The Spirit of the Game[96] - Jeff Sutherland, James O. Coplien, and The Scrum Patterns Group
- Organizational Patterns of Agile Software Development[97] - James O. Coplien, Neil B. Harrison

---

[94]http://www.scrumplop.org
[95]http://scrumbook.org/
[96]https://www.goodreads.com/book/show/45029885-a-scrum-book
[97]https://www.goodreads.com/book/show/756250.Organizational_Patterns_of_Agile_Software_Development

# Open and Inner Source

**As the** Author
**I want** to describe the Open Source development practices
**So that** the reader understands how to get the related benefits within their organization.

## Definitions

We call "**Open Source**," the software with the source code freely available for possible modification and redistribution[98]. From the legal point of view, this is regulated thanks to a user license[99] that allows the source code, blueprint, and design to be used, modified, and shared under defined terms and conditions. Furthermore, the "Open-Source Model" is a decentralized software development model observed in the Open Souce development communities that encourages open collaboration[100].

"**Inner Source**" is a software development strategy that applies the open source software development model within organizations to develop proprietary software[101]. InnerSource can help establish an open source culture within an organization while retaining the source code only for internal use. The term was coined by Tim O'Reilly, founder of O'Reilly Media, in 2000, describing it

---

[98]Open-source Software: https://en.wikipedia.org/wiki/Open-source_software
[99]Open Source Licenses: https://en.wikipedia.org/wiki/Open-source_license
[100]The cathedral and the bazaar - Eric S. Raymond: https://en.wikipedia.org/wiki/The_Cathedral_and_the_Bazaar
[101]InnerSource: https://en.wikipedia.org/wiki/Inner_source

as: "the use of open source development techniques within the corporation[102].

The benefits observed when adopting this model vary from a faster Time-to-Market, reduced development costs, better code quality, more reusability, better and flexible utilization of developers, and enhanced knowledge management. In addition, companies using this approach generally showed better resiliency and agility than structured and siloed organizations[103].

# Inner Source Practices

While the Open Source Model will be clear and familiar for any company developing an Open Source project, the practices that could be transferred to an internal proprietary development are not immediate to most closed-source software firms. This section will go through some of the typical Inner Source practices.

Inner Source is not a defined method like Scrum, which specifies roles, events, and artifacts. Instead, Inner Source is best described as a set of practices. Typically Inner Source includes:

- Access to all development assets on a global scale, including code, specifications, and documentation.
- The freedom for anybody to review and propose code contributions.
- Independent peer review and evaluation of developer community member contributions.
- Informal contact methods include mailing lists, chat rooms, and forums.
- Self-selection of tasks, enabling developers to pick out areas of the software they think they can enhance or bugs to correct.

---

[102]InnerSource: An Open Source Approach to Community Culture, Ben Van't Ende: https://ageofpeers.com/2016/05/09/an-open-source-approach-to-community-culture/

[103]Inner Source Definition, Benefits, and Challenges - Capraro, Maximilian; Riehle, Dirk: https://opus4.kobv.de/opus4-fau/files/7544/capraro-riehle_inner-source-survey.pdf

- Frequent releases and early feedback to make the project active and progressing rapidly.

## Transparency

In Open Source development, the process is transparent and typically available to anybody who wants to participate. The product creation is also community-based. Transparency is crucial, but it's not always easy to implement. Sharing code and development responsibilities may not be something that developers and managers are comfortable with. However, it is crucial to make all development artifacts completely accessible through supporting infrastructure. This infrastructure includes a source code repository, a wiki for knowledge sharing, a mailing list or a forum, and a chat tool for synchronous communication. Developers wouldn't be able to "lurk" and contribute to projects without this transparency.

## Bottom-up features

In contrast to conventional methods, where requirements are determined before implementation, in open source development, requirements are frequently described as expressed post-factum. Features are contributed by developers who, from their perspective, see particular lacking capabilities. This bottom-up approach adheres to the "scratch your own itch" approach, which Eric Raymond, in his book "The Cathedral and the Bazaar[104]" mentions as one of the rules for developing outstanding open source software. In the last decade, organizations like Red Hat and Google and significant initiatives like the Linux kernel and Android have used this strategy on a planetary scale with excellent results.

---

[104]https://en.wikipedia.org/wiki/The_Cathedral_and_the_Bazaar

## Peer Reviewed Development and Deployment

Although peer review is not unique to open source development, the massive scale on which it occurs is unique to open source projects, as a reflection of Linus Torvards's Law, "Given enough eyeballs, all bugs are shallow." "Release early. Release often" is another motto frequently heard in open source groups that encourages early feedback on new work.

What happened to the previously described approach where anyone could create a new feature and decide whether it was a good idea? In many organizations, the peer review approach is employed to assess the code's quality and obtain peer approval for the new code in the project's trunk.

## Modularity

The modularity of a product is another aspect to consider. Even though modularity is a desirable quality for all software, community-based development places a premium on it. First, it enables engineers to concentrate on studying a portion of the total code to which they may subsequently make a valuable contribution. Second, it makes parallel development easier. When contributions are checked in multiple developers can work on various project components simultaneously without encountering merge conflicts.

## Tools

The development tools' availability and a certain level of standardization are needed. Disparate and incompatible technologies could make it challenging to share contributions or even to create and execute the software on specific platforms. In addition, given the level of innovation, some tools might become obsolete quickly.

Many companies find it challenging to balance the freedom of experimenting with new tools and the need for an overall harmonization. Regardless of the technology or brand, any organization must have synchronous and asynchronous communication tools, co-design and brainstorming platforms, task tracking, and code versioning.

## Knowledge Management

The cost of onboarding a new contributor to a project is directly proportional to the number of random voluntary contributions they will get. Therefore, it's vital to organize the specifications and the documentation in a way that is easy to consult in a self-service fashion. In addition, established practices must be codified in an easy-to-access way, like coding standards, naming conventions, working agreements, and general rules.

# Further readings

- The cathedral and the bazaar - Eric S. Raymond: https://en. wikipedia.org/wiki/The_Cathedral_and_the_Bazaar
- "InnerSource: An Open Source Approach to Community Culture" - Ben Van't Ende: https://ageofpeers.com/2016/05/09/an-open-source-approach-to-community-culture/
- "Inner Source Definition, Benefits, and Challenges" - Capraro, Maximilian; Riehle, Dirk: https://opus4.kobv.de/opus4-fau/files/7544/capraro-riehle_inner-source-survey.pdf
- "Inner Source—Adopting Open Source Development Practices within Organizations: A Tutorial" - Klaas-Jan Stol, Brian Fitzgerald: https://ulir.ul.ie/bitstream/handle/10344/4443/Stol_2014_inner.pdf

# Case Study: Ubuntu

The time frame of this case study is comprised of between 2006 to 2015. For these nearly ten years, I was involved in the project as a Community Leader with the Italian and International communities[105]. I'm aware of changes after departing the project, and I am sure things will change again. This story doesn't want to be a detailed description of things but just a testimonial of what I've seen with my eyes, hoping it will inspire others.

## The Ubuntu Project

The Ubuntu project was founded in 2004 by Mark Shuttleworth[106], a South African-British entrepreneur, to build an operating system based on the Debian Linux distribution and composed mainly of free and open-source software.

The Ubuntu word comes from Bantu, a language spoken in central and south Africa, meaning "humanity," sometimes translated as "I am what I am because we all are" or "humanity towards others."

Since the beginning, the Ubuntu project has been backed by Canonical Ltd, the company offering professional services on the Ubuntu platform founded and led by Mark Shuttleworth himself as CEO.

When, in 2004, Shuttleworth founded Ubuntu, he was already well known. In 1999 he sold his company Thawte, which specialized in digital certificates and Internet security, to VeriSign for 575 Million USD. Later, in 2002, he became the second space tourist in history and the first African from an independent country to travel to space.[107]. Mark chaired the Ubuntu project from the beginning with the title "Benevolent Dictator for Life[108]."

---

[105]https://wiki.ubuntu.com/PaoloSammicheli
[106]https://en.wikipedia.org/wiki/Mark_Shuttleworth
[107]https://en.wikipedia.org/wiki/Mark_Shuttleworth
[108]https://en.wikipedia.org/wiki/Benevolent_dictator_for_life

## The Ubuntu Promise

Initially, Ubuntu was distributed with CDs and available to download online.

| Ubuntu 7.10 | Ubuntu 8.10 | Ubuntu 12.10 |

**Ubuntu CD, source Wikimedia Commons**

The CD cover contained the Ubuntu Promise, with a synthesis of the project goals:

- Ubuntu will always be free of charge, including enterprise releases and security updates.
- Ubuntu comes with full commercial support from Canonical and hundreds of companies worldwide.
- Ubuntu includes the best translations and accessibility infrastructure that the free software community offers.
- Ubuntu CDs contain only free software applications; we encourage you to use free and open-source software, improve it and pass it on.

## Ubuntu ecosystem

Ubuntu developed an ecosystem[109] of different editions:

- Ubuntu Desktop[110] - A complete desktop Linux operating system, freely available with community and professional support.

---

[109]https://wiki.ubuntu.com/DerivativeTeam/Derivatives
[110]http://www.ubuntu.com/desktop

- Ubuntu Server[111] - The most popular server Linux in the cloud and data center, with five years of guaranteed free upgrades.
- Ubuntu Core[112] - a lean operating system for the Internet of Things.
- Ubuntu Cloud[113] - optimized and certified server images for partners like Amazon AWS, Microsoft Azure, Google Cloud Platform, Oracle, Rackspace, and IBM Cloud.

The project also includes different "flavors[114]," distinct experiences relative to the "plain" Ubuntu Desktop, like a particular desktop environment, a specific intended use case, or a particular theme. All flavors of Ubuntu use the same repository for downloading updates, so the same set of packages is available regardless of the flavor initially installed. The Ubuntu flavors include:

- Kubuntu[115] - a KDE Plasma Workspace experience for home and office use.
- Lubuntu[116] - a light, fast, and modern Ubuntu flavor using LXQt as its default desktop environment.
- Ubuntu Kylin[117] - tuned to the needs of Chinese users, providing a thoughtful and elegant Chinese experience out-of-the-box.
- Ubuntu Studio[118] - a multimedia content creation flavor aimed at the audio, video, and graphic professional.
- Xubuntu[119] - an easy-to-use operating system based on the Xfce desktop environment.

---

[111] http://www.ubuntu.com/server
[112] https://www.ubuntu.com/core
[113] https://ubuntu.com/download/cloud
[114] https://wiki.ubuntu.com/UbuntuFlavors
[115] https://www.kubuntu.org/
[116] https://lubuntu.me/
[117] https://www.ubuntukylin.com/
[118] https://ubuntustudio.org/
[119] https://xubuntu.org/

# The Ubuntu community

When I joined the Ubuntu community, it was composed of around 3000 contributors, with only 200 people being Canonical employees. With such a large number of volunteers, topics like engagement, morale, and commitment were vital and incredibly challenging. Still today, after years of learning about leadership, I consider an environment like that the **Formula 1** of leadership and community engagement.

The community was welcoming and engaging. There I met incredible talents well-known and respected internationally. But still, I counter low ego and an authentic sense of community.

The Code of Conduct was one pilar of the Ubuntu Community culture [120]. The first formal step to join the community was to digitally sign this document with a cryptographic key[121] as a commitment to following it[122]. Following the Ubuntu Code of Conduct's last version, published in 2012.

# Ubuntu Code of Conduct v2.0

Ubuntu is about showing humanity to one another: the word itself captures the spirit of being human.

We want a productive, happy and agile community that can welcome new ideas in a complex field, improve every process every year, and foster collaboration between groups with very different needs, interests and skills.

We gain strength from diversity, and actively seek participation from those who enhance it. This code of conduct exists to ensure that diverse groups collaborate to mutual advantage and enjoyment. We will challenge prejudice that could jeopardise the participation of any person in the project.

---

[120]https://ubuntu.com/community/code-of-conduct
[121]https://help.ubuntu.com/community/GnuPrivacyGuardHowto
[122]https://wiki.ubuntu.com/Membership

The Code of Conduct governs how we behave in public or in private whenever the project will be judged by our actions. We expect it to be honoured by everyone who represents the project officially or informally, claims affiliation with the project, or participates directly. We strive to:

## Be considerate

Our work will be used by other people, and we in turn will depend on the work of others. Any decision we take will affect users and colleagues, and we should consider them when making decisions.

## Be respectful

Disagreement is no excuse for poor manners. We work together to resolve conflict, assume good intentions and do our best to act in an empathic fashion. We don't allow frustration to turn into a personal attack. A community where people feel uncomfortable or threatened is not a productive one.

## Take responsibility for our words and our actions

We can all make mistakes; when we do, we take responsibility for them. If someone has been harmed or offended, we listen carefully and respectfully, and work to right the wrong.

## Be collaborative

What we produce is a complex whole made of many parts, it is the sum of many dreams. Collaboration between teams that each have their own goal and vision is essential; for the whole to be more than the sum of its parts, each part must make an effort to understand the whole.

Collaboration reduces redundancy and improves the quality of our work. Internally and externally, we celebrate good collaboration.

Wherever possible, we work closely with upstream projects and others in the free software community to coordinate our efforts. We prefer to work transparently and involve interested parties as early as possible.

## Value decisiveness, clarity and consensus

Disagreements, social and technical, are normal, but we do not allow them to persist and fester leaving others uncertain of the agreed direction. We expect participants in the project to resolve disagreements constructively. When they cannot, we escalate the matter to structures with designated leaders to arbitrate and provide clarity and direction.

## Ask for help when unsure

Nobody is expected to be perfect in this community. Asking questions early avoids many problems later, so questions are encouraged, though they may be directed to the appropriate forum. Those who are asked should be responsive and helpful.

## Step down considerately

When somebody leaves or disengages from the project, we ask that they do so in a way that minimises disruption to the project. They should tell people they are leaving and take the proper steps to ensure that others can pick up where they left off.

## Leadership, authority and responsibility

We all lead by example, in debate and in action. We encourage new participants to feel empowered to lead, to take action, and to experiment when they feel innovation could improve the project. Leadership can be exercised by anyone simply by taking action, there is no need to wait for recognition when the opportunity to lead presents itself.

## Delegation from the top

Responsibility for the project starts with the "benevolent dictator", who delegates specific responsibilities and the corresponding authority to a series of teams, councils and individuals, starting with the Community Council ("CC"). That Council or its delegated representative will arbitrate in any dispute.

We are a meritocracy; we delegate decision making, governance and leadership from senior bodies to the most able and engaged candidates.

## Support for delegation is measured

Nominations to the boards and councils are at the discretion of the Community Council, however the Community Council will seek the input of the community before confirming appointments.

Leadership is not an award, right, or title; it is a privilege, a responsibility and a mandate. A leader will only retain their authority as long as they retain the support of those who delegated that authority to them.

## We value discussion, data and decisiveness

We gather opinions, data and commitments from concerned parties before taking a decision. We expect leaders to help teams come to a decision in a reasonable time, to seek guidance or be willing to take the decision themselves when consensus is lacking, and to take responsibility for implementation.

The poorest decision of all is no decision: clarity of direction has value in itself. Sometimes all the data are not available, or consensus is elusive. A decision must still be made. There is no guarantee of a perfect decision every time - we prefer to err, learn, and err less in future than to postpone action indefinitely.

We recognise that the project works better when we trust the teams closest to a problem to make the decision for the project. If we learn of a decision that we disagree with, we can engage the relevant team to find common ground, and failing that, we have a governance structure that can review the decision. Ultimately, if a decision has been taken by the people responsible for it, and is supported by the project governance, it will stand. None of us expects to agree with every decision, and we value highly the willingness to stand by the project and help it deliver even on the occasions when we ourselves may prefer a different route.

## Open meritocracy

We invite anybody, from any company, to participate in any aspect of the project. Our community is open, and any responsibility can be carried by any contributor who demonstrates the required capacity and competence.

## Teamwork

A leader's foremost goal is the success of the team. "A virtuoso is judged by their actions; a leader is judged by the actions of their team." A leader knows when to act and when to step back. They know when to delegate work, and when to take it upon themselves.

## Credit

A good leader does not seek the limelight, but celebrates team members for the work they do. Leaders may be more visible than members of the team, good ones use that visibility to highlight the great work of others.

## Courage and considerateness

Leadership occasionally requires bold decisions that will not be widely understood, consensual or popular. We value the courage to take such decisions, because they enable the project as a whole to move forward faster than we could if we required complete consensus. Nevertheless, boldness demands considerateness; take bold decisions, but do so mindful of the challenges they present for others, and work to soften the impact of those decisions on them. Communicating changes and their reasoning clearly and early on is as important as the implementation of the change itself.

## Conflicts of interest

We expect leaders to be aware when they are conflicted due to employment or other projects they are involved in, and abstain or delegate decisions that may be seen to be self-interested. We expect that everyone who participates in the project does so with the goal of making life better for its users.

When in doubt, ask for a second opinion. Perceived conflicts of interest are important to address; as a leader, act to ensure that decisions are credible even if they must occasionally be unpopular, difficult or favourable to the interests of one group over another.

This code is not exhaustive or complete. It is not a rulebook; it serves to distil our common understanding of a collaborative, shared environment and goals. We expect it to be followed in spirit as much as in the letter.

# Release Cycle

The Ubuntu release cycle[123] was organized with a six-month cadence, releasing every year in April and October. The version numbering follows the schema of YY.MM, so the release of April 2012 would be numbered 12.04. Every two years, starting from April 2006, there's a version called LTS, Long Term Support, with five years of publicly available support and security updates. The other version had support for 18 months instead and implied an

---

[123]https://ubuntu.com/about/release-cycle

upgrade to the new release every six months. Compared to the other operating system Ubuntu was competing on the desktop platform, it was four times as frequent in 2006, reduced to twice as frequent in 2015, when both Microsoft and Apple shortened their release cycle.

Operating systems release cycle comparison

Each release of Ubuntu has a development codename, assigned just before the ending of the previous release, with the "adjective – animal" scheme using the same initial, which changed in a progressive order (e.g., Gutsy Gibbon, Hardy Heron, Intrepid Ibex, etc.).

Internally, Ubuntu implemented continuous integration with a daily build cycle. During the time window "night" in US East, West, and European time, the CD image was rebuilt with the day's source code commits and executed with the automated tests. (I don't recall exactly when, but approximately between 8 pm - 10 pm pacific time, hence 11 pm - 1 am us eastern and 5 am - 7 am central Europe.) Furthermore, many developers followed the "Eating your own dog food[124]" practice, using the unstable under-development version on their laptops to detect bugs and integration problems.

## Tools

The central platform to support Ubuntu development is Launch-pad[125], a web application developed by Canonical Ltd and hosting many other projects.

---

[124]https://en.wikipedia.org/wiki/Eating_your_own_dog_food
[125]https://launchpad.net

Launchpad provided for each project multiple tools:

- Project Home page, with information on the project leaders and membership
- Source Code repository, including the contributions approval process
- Package repository to automate update distribution
- Bug Tracking tool supports crowdsourced bug reproduction, confirmation, and resolution.
- Blueprints with the specs of the current developments
- Translations
- Question and Answers

At that time, many aspects of Launchpad were very innovative. All the efforts were directed towards simplifying the contribution to increase community engagement and growth. For example, the translation could be done directly from the web interface, allowing new members to suggest a translation even for a single sentence. Compared to the other projects that required downloading the entire string files and editing locally with a text editor, this approach significantly simplified the initial contribution and attracted average users. On the other hand, although the Debian project had almost the same software base, it mainly attracted only power users and seasoned developers.

To manage identity and security, Ubuntu, like any other Linux distribution, used Gnu Pretty Guard[126]: a free and open cryptographic system that allows to encrypt and digitally sign files. The

---

[126]https://gnupg.org

synchronous communication was through IRC[127], a textual chat used by most other OS projects. In addition, asynchronous communication flowed through the Forum[128] and the Mailing Lists[129]. Finally, the Wiki website[130] hosted the documentation, developed collaboratively by the entire community.

## Packages organization

The software composing an Ubuntu system is distributed with a system called Debian Packages[131]. Distributing the software with Debian Packages allowed automatic installation and upgrades, automatic dependencies resolution, and a high reusability of software components across different products. This highly modular approach was one of the critical enabling elements that allowed Ubuntu to have many editions and flavors without multiplying the effort.

The packages are organized in Web Repositories[132], containing the latest package version so that users can download them.

Ubuntu divided the software into four repositories:

1. **Main** - Canonical-supported free and open-source software.
2. **Universe** - Community-maintained free and open-source software.
3. **Restricted** - Proprietary drivers for devices.
4. **Multiverse** - Software restricted by copyright or legal issues.

The developers with writing rights in the Main repository are called "Ubuntu Core Developers" and are divided into teams focused on a specific group of packages, like:

---

[127]https://wiki.ubuntu.com/IRC/ChannelList
[128]https://ubuntuforums.org
[129]https://lists.ubuntu.com
[130]https://wiki.ubuntu.com
[131]https://wiki.debian.org/Packaging/Intro
[132]https://help.ubuntu.com/community/Repositories/Ubuntu

- Ubuntu Desktop Developers[133]
- Ubuntu Kernel Uploaders[134]
- Ubuntu GNOME Developers[135]
- Ubuntu Mozilla Uploaders[136]
- Ubuntu Server Developers[137]
- And many other

The complete list[138] is available in the Ubuntu Wiki.

When I was contributing to the project, most of the Ubuntu Core Developers were Canonical employees. The maintainers of the Universe repository, instead, were almost entirely volunteers, with some exceptions, and named "Master of the Universe" or MOTU[139].

## Ubuntu Developer Summit

The project had a semi-annual meeting called Ubuntu Developer Summits[140], also commonly known as UDS, that happened from 2004 to 2012.

These events took place shortly after the release of a new operating system version, that is twice a year[141], and it was the occasion to discuss the last release and what to include in the following one.

During development, each release[142] of Ubuntu had a code name using the "adjective – animal" scheme with the same initial, which changed in progressive order:

---

[133]https://launchpad.net/~ubuntu-desktop
[134]https://launchpad.net/~ubuntu-kernel-uploaders
[135]https://launchpad.net/~ubuntu-gnome-dev
[136]https://launchpad.net/~ubuntu-mozilla-uploaders
[137]https://launchpad.net/~ubuntu-server-dev
[138]https://wiki.ubuntu.com/UbuntuDevelopers#Ubuntu_Developers_.28from_delegated_teams.29
[139]https://wiki.ubuntu.com/MOTU
[140]https://wiki.ubuntu.com/DeveloperSummit
[141]https://wiki.ubuntu.com/Releases
[142]https://wiki.ubuntu.com/Releases

- Ubuntu 7.10: Gutsy Gibbon
- Ubuntu 8.04: Hardy Heron
- Ubuntu 8.10: Intrepid Ibex
- Ubuntu 9.04: Jaunty Jackalope
- etc.

The animal used in the code name was also the mascot of the related UDS. The code name announcement for a release was a special moment; Mark Shuttleworth maintained it secret and declared it via his blog, revealing other details such as the release's objectives and the date and location of the following UDS.

The UDS was a considerably big conference, with attendees of over 600, with the duration of one week, from Monday to Friday, organized following the Open Space Technology[143] format, described in general terms later in this chapter.

Open Space means that the conference did not have a predefined program; each participant could suggest an hour-long session and put it into the agenda. This also means that the following day's schedule changed continuously, adapting to new emerging ideas and integrating with the most exciting topics.

The sessions were divided into Tracks: Desktop, Server, Foundation, Community, UX, etc. Each track had an easily recognizable Track Leader with a unique T-shirt, ensuring the sessions were planned harmoniously.

---

[143]https://en.wikipedia.org/wiki/Open_Space_Technology

PHOTO BY GRAHAM BINNS

Some sessions, like the "Community Roundtables," had the agenda emerge from the debate to encourage the flow of discussion. They were similar to Lean Coffees[144]. The substantial difference was that, while in a Lean Coffee, each topic had an exact time slot, usually 10 minutes. In a Community Roundtable, the matter was thoroughly explored using a "Popcorn Discussion" model. As with popcorn, which is to be removed from the fire when it stops popping, then when talks started decreasing and interest fell, the session leader closed the topic and introduced the following.

What impressed me was that all these organizational rules, models, and formulas were not explained or documented: the leaders and the majority of participants did so, and everyone behaved accordingly. All this created a unique – unusual – atmosphere.

---

[144]http://leancoffee.org

Ubuntu Developer Summit - December 2008

## Open Space

In a typical conference format the whole program is defined and published before the event. However, a more accessible and emerging format is increasingly being applied to companies traditionally more inclined to structure any situation, such as banks.

The best-known format for organizing an unstructured conference (also known as unconference) is called Open Space Technology[145]. It is based on four principles:

1. Whoever comes is the right people
2. Whatever happens is the only thing that could have
3. Whenever it starts is the right time
4. When it's over, it's over

The only rule in the format is called the "law of two feet," that is:

> "If at any time during our time together you find yourself in any situation where you are neither learning nor contributing, use your two feet and go someplace else where you can be more productive."

---

[145]https://en.wikipedia.org/wiki/Open_Space_Technology

It is easy to understand how these principles and this simple rule create complex, dynamic, and spontaneous behavior.

A facilitator directs the event, or more than one if the conference is enormous.

Before the conference begins, an empty program grid is prepared, showing the planning's available spaces and the time slots. The grid is generally analogical, set up on a wall covered in sticky notes; in crowded conferences, you can use a software tool accessible from a PC and mobile.

At the beginning of the Open Space, a "market" moment is organized. All the participants gather in a single room, and the facilitator explains the principles, the law, and the practical rules for using the tools and the available spaces. Then you leave some time to allow the schedule to fill up for at least the first day of the event. If you use an analog program on a wall, every proponent presents their session in a few words (less than 1 minute).

**Program of POCamp 2016**

At that point, the event begins, and a sort of "organized chaos" creates magic, generating exciting and productive conversations.

The proponents of each session act as facilitators of the sessions themselves and worry that the times are strictly respected to avoid overlapping sessions and collect the synthesis of the produced material.

Usually, a collective final moment is used to share what they liked the most in rotation and the feedback to better organize it the following time.

POCamp 2016 final retrospective

## Practices used in UDS

In this section, I will list the practices refined over the years in the UDS. But, as described before, it's not necessarily the current state of practices since they evolve continuously.

The **schedule** was kept on a proprietary software product called **summit.ubuntu.com**, which today is used for a different purpose. The program was divided into Tracks (for example, Desktop, Server, Mobile, Community, etc.); each track had a leader, clearly identifiable by a unique shirt, which served as session facilitator. To avoid duplication of sessions, he received notification of each new session. All participants were invited to speak with the track's leader to ensure that the topic was not already present in other sessions. Proposals began a few days before, so there was already material to cover the first days at the conference's opening. The rest of the days were filled with new proposals that gradually emerged during the works.

Half Day Program of UDS, May 2011

The **spaces** were organized very well. There were two projectors in each room where the sessions were held, one available to project something from the proponent's PC, such as slides or other material, to see the **meeting notes** of the session. Each session aimed at having actions at its end, so the approach was very pragmatic. Using tools that allowed the simultaneous editing of a file, all participants collaboratively updated the report of what was discussed with the list of actions. The tools used were Gobby[146] at first and then the most modern Etherpad[147] later. With the meeting notes projection, all the participants, even those with no PC, could see what was transcribed and suggest changes or ideas in real time. Also, those who arrived late would immediately see what had been discussed up to that point.

---

[146]http://gobby.github.io/
[147]http://etherpad.org/

The actions that emerged from each session were tracked on Launch-pad[148], another software developed internally within Ubuntu to manage the development of the project, in a component called Blueprint[149]. The participants voluntarily took on these tasks, and a burn-down chart[150] was automatically generated on them, indicating the progress on a site called **status.ubuntu.com**, today not online anymore.

It was also possible to participate remotely in each session. Remote participants could listen to the conversation with audio streaming and ask questions through the IRC[151] chat.

Each session could have different objectives: some were about past developments to suggest actions of improvement, others dedicated to discussions about the future or to plan the works to come.

Mark Shuttleworth opened the week with a Keynote speech in which he shared the vision for the next release. The after-lunch time slot, however, was reserved for various kinds of Keynote talks. Having a motivating talk at the most critical time, just after lunch, was an intelligent practice as it allowed us to focus more on the work of the evening. The community manager Jono Bacon[152], today not involved anymore in the project, traditionally animated the closing slot of the last day: the feedback and greetings moment.

## Quality and Testing

To get a high-quality standard, Ubuntu organized the QA Team[153]. Differently from many corporations I know, the QA Team wasn't responsible for testing the platform but for developing, organizing, and maintaining all the quality tools for the entire platform. This approach reminds me of Spotify's Engineering Culture 1[154] video,

---

[148]https://launchpad.net/
[149]https://launchpad.net/+tour/feature-tracking
[150]https://en.wikipedia.org/wiki/Burn_down_chart
[151]https://en.wikipedia.org/wiki/Internet_Relay_Chat
[152]https://www.jonobacon.com
[153]https://wiki.ubuntu.com/QATeam/
[154]https://engineering.atspotify.com/2014/03/spotify-engineering-culture-part-1/

where they show their self-service model, where for a team working on internal needs «Enabling is more important than serving.»

Ubuntu used a combined approach of manual and automatic testing, where manual testing was organized in a crowdsourcing way, meaning that anybody from the power-users community was enabled to test new features and report bugs.

Bug triaging was also a crowdsourced effort that involved thousands of contributors.

## Testing Crown sourcing

During the fall of 2010, I participated in organizing the Local Community Team crown sourced testing[155]. This activity, meant to be a complimentary crowdsourced testing approach, was intended to create in Local Communities group of testers of the interim releases that happen every major development release (Alpha, Beta, and Candidate releases). Approaching crowdsourcing testing as a team increased the quality and the speed of the bug reported. The main difference with pure unstructured crowdsourced testing was that another LoCo QA Team Member was asked to reproduce and confirm the reported bugs. This also increased the diversity of the testing thank to the fact that the Local Communities involved were not English speakers. The work was organized in a "Pull" fashion, where volunteers adopted specific platforms and flavors.

ISO Testing

| Nome | Ubuntu Desktop | | Kubuntu Desktop | | Xubuntu Desktop | | Lubuntu Desktop | | Edubuntu | |
|---|---|---|---|---|---|---|---|---|---|---|
| | x86 | amd 64 | x86 | amd 64 | x86 | amd 64 | x86 | amd 64 | x86 | amd 64 |
| PaoloSammicheli | x | | | | | | | | | |
| AlbertoRusso | | | | | x | | | | | |
| ClaudioArseni | x | x | x | | | | | | | |
| FabioMarconi | | x | | | | | | | | |
| SergioZanchetta | x | | | | | x | | | | |
| RiccardoAngelino | | | x | | | | | | | |
| MorrisCavestro | | | | | x | | | | | |
| FrancescoRuvolo | | | x | | | x | | x | | |
| AlessandroFrancia | | | | | | | x | | | |
| PaoloRotolo | | | x | | | | | | | |

---

[155]https://wiki.ubuntu.com/Testing/LoCoTeam

Using a multi-language testing approach also improved the translations and an effort spanning all time zones, implementing a "follow the sun" development spanning 24 hours. In addition, the International QA Team was providing a tool called "ISO Tracker" that alerted by email the volunteers of the availability of a new version of the adopted images and was the repository to collect test results and the list of bugs detected.

More details of the organization are available on the Testing LoCo Team wiki[156] page and the Testing ISO Procedures[157].

## Conclusion

The Open Source Model implemented in Ubuntu in the described period is a complex and impressive implementation that allowed the development of an extensive software collection like an Operating System distributed in 5 editions and more than four flavors on multiple hardware platforms (Intel, AMD, Arm) with a number of people that is a fraction between 100 and 1000 times smaller than what we see in proprietary software companies.

---

[156]https://wiki.ubuntu.com/Testing/LoCoTeam
[157]https://wiki.ubuntu.com/Testing/ISO/Procedures

The Ubuntu development, thanks to highly motivated employees, a disciplined approach, strong leadership, and an enormous volunteer contribution, allowed a development cycle that today, in 2022, is impressive, and in 2006 was just incredible.

With today's technological advancement, this development model could be combined with the newest remote working tools to dramatically increase a company's productivity.

# In Practice

**As the** Author
**I want** to detail the method, composed by specific practices useful in AI development
**So that** this book will help people to develop AI.

This chapter collects the patterns and the practices to effectively develop AI-Based applications using Agile and Scrum. If you do not clearly understand the basics, I recommend reading the previous part, The Fundamentals.

# Scrum in Artificial Intelligence

**As the** Author
**I want** to introduce the topic of Scrum and AI
**So that** I start introducing what needs to be considered
from traditional software development

The first obvious question would be: why should developing machine learning applications be different from any other software development approach?

We introduced these differences in the Fundamentals Part in the "The challenges to developing AI" Chapter. To recap, the main aspects we should consider are:

- Black Box problem: The algorithm is generated with training, so it's hard, if not impossible, to understand and debug it.
- Testing: The behavior of the models is "intelligent," so it's hard, if not impossible, to automatically test it with traditional, non-intelligent systems.
- Data Quality: Often, that is only discovered during development. This adds uncertainty and risks.
- Data Drift, Concept Drift. Your production model would be stale at some point. Therefore, you will need to monitor and retrain your models after release.
- Estimation: Model Accuracy is challenging, if not impossible, to be forecast, so estimation is complex, if not impossible.
- Project Funding: The pace of Innovation makes it hard, if not impossible, to forecast the product lifecycle, and ROI is most of the time a pure guess.

- Ethics: A new set of problems like biases, discrimination, and social concerns are very different from traditional software development.
- Cybersecurity: AI-specific threats, in addition to the generic security concerns, make it even more challenging
- Regulation: Specific emerging policies that, in addition to the existing one specific for each industry, increase complexity and uncertainty even more.

# Tweaking the Scrum Structure

Given the previously described problems and concerns, should we modify the structure of Scrum?

When a Scrum Master feels the need to tweak the elements of the Scrum Guide, it means they don't understand Scrum.

My advice is always to maintain the 353 structure: 3 Roles, 5 Events, 3 Artifacts. From what I learned from Jeff Sutherland, the Scrum elements are meant to reinforce each other. Changing the Scrum fundamental elements will lead you to a place of undesired side effects.

When there's a particular need, the extensive library of Scrum Patterns, with 135 patterns in the Scrum Book Patlets[158] only, will be for sure a source of inspiration.

# Empiricism and Feedback

The pillars of Scrum, the same as Empiricism, are:

Transparency, Inspection, and Adaptation.

---

[158]http://scrumbook.org/book-outline/patlets.html

Empiricism is a theory that states that knowledge comes primarily from experience. It emphasizes the role of empirical evidence in the formation of ideas[159].

For this reason, in Scrum, we invest a lot of time asking for feedback, understanding it, and incorporating it into the current development.

We define the people who can help us with inspecting and adapting as "Stakeholders." They can be clients, users, experts, colleagues, managers, and so on. We regularly show at the Sprint Reviews to the Stakeholders what is produced during the Sprint, the Increment, to hear their opinion and feedback.

Most of the time, with AI-based applications, Stakeholders are interested in what you do, and they probably ask you to see it. The problem is that they don't know more than you do if the Increment does fit the purpose. You need to find the feedback elsewhere.

The good news is that the feedback you need is just there under your nose: it's in the data!

The data in the production system, with the real behavior, contains most of the time all the feedback you need. So you have to inspect it regularly and incorporate what you learn in the development as soon as you can, implementing an iterative and incremental development, like with the "Mona Lisa" in the following image[160]:

---

[159] https://en.wikipedia.org/wiki/Empiricism
[160] Image from https://www.jonahgroup.com/blog/agile-development-and-the-mona-lisa/

Based on empiricism, iterative and incremental product development allows risk reduction at the beginning, split the return of investment in multiple releases, and understands user needs thanks to continuous feedback.

# Product Backlog

The Product Backlog Items (PBI) are mostly outcome-driven, not output-driven. Given the complexity of the topic, you can't find on a PBI the detailed description of what to do, but more what we intend to achieve. And you iterate until you get it. We have seen this approach already, for example, in the Spotify Engineering Culture 2[161].

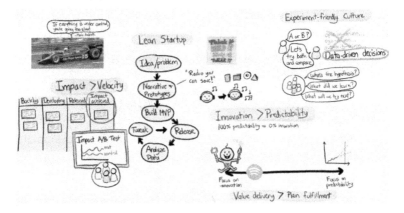

New Product Backlog Items come both from top-down requests and bottom-up ideas. In traditional software development, the relation between the team proposed PBI and stakeholders favors the latter. They are those who ask for more stuff. With AI, most of the time, the need for co-creation is significant, and the ratio of requests from business and ideas from developers tend to be equal. Also, Business people alone know what they want to achieve, the Outcome, but have no idea of what they want, the Output. For example, with a

---

[161]https://engineering.atspotify.com/2014/09/20/spotify-engineering-culture-part-2/

conversational AI, stakeholders may ask for a general Outcome like "can we offer this service through our AI customer rep?" rather than specific questions on what kind of request the AI would be capable of managing.

## Outcome Driven Development

I call this kind of approach "Outcome-Driven Development," in contrast with the traditional "output-driven development." In what this is different? With output-driven development, the more Acceptance Criteria a story has, the better from a developer's perspective. Acceptance Criteria bring clarity when you are developing a specific output.

With Outcome-Driven Development, the Acceptance Criteria represent the constraints we need to consider, nothing else. For this reason, the fewer constraints we have, the better. It will be easier for the Developers to propose an idea that easily fits a Sprint time with a limited number of limitations.

# Outcome Driven Development

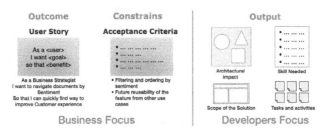

It's common to iterate the same user stories changing only the Acceptance Criteria or the proposed solution. Sometimes there may be the need for concurrent development (Set-Based Design Pattern[162]) for very complex problems. Product Backlog Refinement will be critical for clarification and constrains definition, so we

---

[162]http://scrumbook.org/value-stream/set-based-design.html

need to allocate proper Refinement time for brainstorming and co-design between Developers and Stakeholders. The 2017 Scrum Guide suggested up to 10% of the Sprint time. I found out that this percentage is used entirely in some AI teams and sometimes even exceeded, and it looks very functional in this continuous co-design context.

# Sprint Planning

Given the complexity and the uncertainty of the development, Sprint Planning is gut-feeling driven, and teams pull enough Ready Stories to have enough work for the next Sprint. No forecast, commitment, story points, and velocity like in traditional software development. I've seen teams tracking progress based on what they achieved rather than what they think will succeed in the next Sprint. I rarely have seen a burn-down chart, if not for midterm goals, updated at the end of each Sprint. Scrum Zelots consider Story Points and burn-down charts vital. Finally, with the Scrum Guide 2020[163], this behavior is deemed to be acceptable, and the importance of Empiricism over the forecasting is stressed out:

> Various practices exist to forecast progress, like burn-downs, burn-ups, or cumulative flows. While proven useful, these do not replace the importance of Empiricism. In complex environments, what will happen is unknown. Only what has already happened may be used for forward-looking decision-making.

# Sprint Backlog

The Sprint Backlog is way more emergent than in traditional software development. Mature Teams, instead of creating tasks for

---

[163]https://scrumguides.org

each story, prefer focussing on one or max two outcome-driven PBI with the "Swarming Pattern[164]" and call it DONE when it appears good enough (i.e., we have 95% of accuracy with a significant data set).

There's no black and white if you develop an AI. Well, even with traditional software development, to be honest, and managers tend to forget it.

The majority of the team I coached found it very useful to implement the Interruption Buffer Pattern[165], to fix the bugs as soon they are discovered, and the Scrumming the Scrum Pattern[166]. In this way, they have only one board for improvements, bugs, and PBI/Tasks.

| Stories | Task To Do | Task Doing | Task Done | Story Done |
|---|---|---|---|---|
| Kaizen | ☐ ☐ | | | |
| Buffer | empty | | | |
| Story 1 | ☐☐☐☐ ☐☐☐ | | | |
| Story 2 | ☐☐☐ ☐☐ | | | |

# Sprint Review

Most of the time, the Sprint Review is not just for asking for feedback from Stakeholders and Sponsors: It is also for socializing the feedback we got so far from data and metrics and updating the sponsors, managers, and other team members on what we

[164]http://scrumbook.org/product-organization-pattern-language/development-team/swarming--one-piece-continuous-flow.html
[165]http://scrumbook.org/product-organization-pattern-language/illegitimus-non-interruptus.html
[166]http://scrumbook.org/retrospective-pattern-language/scrumming-the-scrum.html

learned and where we think we are. This fuel the Product Backlog Refinement where the Scrum Team and some stakeholder may co-design new features or evolutions of the existing ones.

Being able to deliver incrementally, and with discipline, increments every Sprint reduces risk and creates the sustainable pace needed to create an environment of productivity and innovation.

The need to enter into technical detail is often reasonable with AI. So I've seen dividing the Sprint Reviews into two parts within the same timebox (two hours for a two-week Sprint): The first part about the business outcomes, and the second part with the learnings from a technical perspective. At the end of the first part, stakeholders from Business and Managers often leave, leaving many technical stakeholders like developers from other teams and experts to learn from the current Increment and eventually provide feedback and suggestions in the second part.

# Engineering Practices

**As the** Author
**I want** to introduce the topic of the Engineering Practices
**So that** the reader can coach his team to high performance and avoid dysfunctional behaviors

## eXtreme Programming

Jeff Sutherland often says that Scrum is one parent of Agile. The Scrum "significant other" that give birth to the Agile Manifesto is considered to be eXtreme Programming[167]:

> Extreme Programming is a discipline of software development based on simplicity, communication, feedback, courage, and respect. It works by bringing the whole team together in simple practices, with enough feedback to enable the team to see where they are and tune the techniques to their unique situation.

In the late nineties, most of the Scrum Team also implemented many engineering practices from XP and vice-versa. As Mike Cohn wrote, "in fact, if you walked in on a team doing one of these processes, you might have a hard time quickly deciding whether you had walked in on a Scrum team or an XP team[168]."

---

[167]https://ronjeffries.com/xprog/book/whatisxp/
[168]https://www.mountaingoatsoftware.com/blog/differences-between-scrum-and-extreme-programming

In the same years, agile practitioners often called it "Scrum/XP" to recognize both methods. With the hype of Agile and Scrum, at the end of the 2000s, the XP name became less prominent in the articles and blogs, even though the practices are extensively used. Somebody told me that the word "Extreme" might scare Managers, so consultants began avoiding it.

I found out that many of the XP practices are useful with AI Development. Specifically, the teams I coached tried:

- Pair Programming[169]
- Test-Driven Development[170]
- Continuous Integration[171]
- Refactoring[172] and Design Improvement
- Small Releases[173]
- System Metaphor[174]

For the first iterations of this book, the eXtreme Programming practices will not be covered more since they are well described elsewhere. Future editions might see an expansion of this section.

## AI Pair Programming

When I was reviewing this chapter, at the end of June 2021, GitHub[175] announced a new project[176] called Copilot[177], consisting of an **AI Pair Programmer** capable of suggesting alternatives of algorithms, writing automated tests, and do some refactoring. The availability is restricted to a limited number of testers at

---

[169]https://en.wikipedia.org/wiki/Pair_programming
[170]https://en.wikipedia.org/wiki/Test-driven_development
[171]https://en.wikipedia.org/wiki/Continuous_integration
[172]https://en.wikipedia.org/wiki/Code_refactoring
[173]https://en.wikipedia.org/wiki/Extreme_programming_practices#Small_releases
[174]https://en.wikipedia.org/wiki/Extreme_programming_practices#System_metaphor
[175]https://github.com
[176]https://github.blog/2021-06-29-introducing-github-copilot-ai-pair-programmer/
[177]https://https://copilot.github.com

the moment. It will be interesting to see and measure how this could improve productivity, reduce technical debt, and change the approach to some eXtreme Programming practices.

## Further Readings

- Extreme Programming Explained: Embrace Change[178] - Kent Beck, Cynthia Andres
- Planning Extreme Programming[179] - Kent Beck, Martin Fowler
- Refactoring: Improving the Design of Existing Code[180] - Martin Fowler, Kent Beck (Contributor), Don Roberts (Contributor)
- Extreme Programming Installed[181] - Ron Jeffries, Ann Anderson, Chet Hendrickson
- Extreme Programming[182] Wiki
- Extreme Programming: A gentle introduction[183] Website

# DevOps

The term DevOps consists of the contraction of the words *Development* and *Operations*. DevOps started in 2009 when Patrick Dubois organized the conference DevOps Days[184].

Many have tried to come up with a definition for DevOps, but today there isn't one universally accepted. The DASA, DevOps Agile Skills Association[185], has formulated six principles[186] which cover well most definitions of DevOps.

---

[178]https://www.goodreads.com/book/show/67833.Extreme_Programming_Explained
[179]https://www.goodreads.com/book/show/67839.Planning_Extreme_Programming
[180]https://www.goodreads.com/book/show/44936.Refactoring
[181]https://www.goodreads.com/book/show/67834.Extreme_Programming_Installed
[182]http://wiki.c2.com/?ExtremeProgramming
[183]http://www.extremeprogramming.org
[184]https://devops.com/the-origins-of-devops-whats-in-a-name/
[185]https://www.devopsagileskills.org
[186]https://www.devopsagileskills.org/dasa-devops-principles/

1. Customer-Centric Action
2. Create with the End in Mind
3. End-to-End Responsibility
4. Cross-Functional Autonomous Teams
5. Continuous Improvement
6. Automate Everything You Can

Jeff Sutherland told me a funny story, claiming that he invented DevOps way before the movement. In the late nineties, one of his teams was struggling with operations because deploying in production was mainly a manual activity, and Operations Engineers wanted to do it themselves without delegating this to the development team. This handover was slowing them down, and it emerged as an impediment from the Retrospective. Jeff, the CTO of the company, got a crazy proposal from the developers: "may we come to work during the night and steal the server? We will take care of it and deploy directly the code at the end of every Sprint." Jeff was amazed by the team's ingenuity and agreed, so they stole overnight the server and installed it at the center of the Scrum Team's room. When Operations Engineers found out the "crime," they went to Sutherland asking for revenge, but he said, "you can have your server back only when you fully automate the deploy, so that nobody would need to ask you permission and lose time." They developed the scripts and got their server back. At the same time, the Scrum Team doubled their velocity, so other Scrum Teams started to ask to Operation Engineers to pair up with them to fully automate the Deployment, which became a norm in the company.

## Further Readings

- The DevOps Handbook: How to Create World-Class Agility, Reliability, and Security in Technology Organizations[187] - Gene Kim, Jez Humble, Patrick Debois, John Willis

---

[187]https://www.goodreads.com/book/show/26083308-the-devops-handbook?from_search=true&from_srp=true&qid=U6R0nkY1SM&rank=1

- The Phoenix Project: A Novel About IT, DevOps, and Helping Your Business Win[188] - Gene Kim, Kevin Behr, George Spafford

# Testing

What happens most of the time, there's no time for testing. Among the development process, testing is considered the *cinderella* of the activities. For example, the Gitlab's 2018 Global Developer Report[189] shows that testing is responsible for more delays than any other part of the development process.

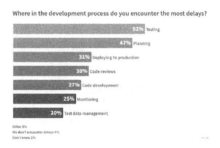

Where in the development process do you encounter the most delays?

| 52% | Testing |
| 47% | Planning |
| 31% | Deploying to production |
| 30% | Code reviews |
| 27% | Code development |
| 25% | Monitoring |
| 20% | Test data management |

Other 5%
We don't encounter delays 4%
Don't know 1%

Why is testing such a frequent bottleneck? Wolfgang Platz, founder of software testing company Tricentis, in his book "Enterprise Continuous Testing" lists many points[190]:

- The vast majority of testing (over 80%) is still performed manually, even more at large enterprise organizations.
- Approximately 67% of the test cases being built, maintained, and executed are redundant and add no value to the testing effort.

---

[188]https://www.goodreads.com/book/show/17255186-the-phoenix-project

[189]https://about.gitlab.com/developer-survey/previous/2018/

[190]Enterprise Continuous Testing (Wolfgang Platz), Pag. 7 "The Speed Problem" - https://www.tricentis.com/enterprise-continuous-testing-book/

- At the organizations with significant test automation, testers spend 17% of their time dealing with false positives and 14% on additional test maintenance tasks.
- Over half of the testers spend 5-15 hours per week dealing with test data, with an average wait time for test data of 2 weeks.
- 84% of testers are routinely delayed by limited test environment access, with an average wait time for test environments of 32 days
- The average regression test suite takes 16.5 days to execute, but the average Sprint length is two weeks, making it impossible to test within the Sprint.

# Agile Testing

Agile recognizes that testing is not a separate phase but an integral part of software development, along with the coding. Agile teams use a "whole-team" approach to "baking quality in" to the software product. Testers on agile teams lend their expertise in eliciting examples of desired behavior from customers, collaborating with the development team to turn those into executable specifications that guide coding. Testing and coding are done incrementally and interactively, building up each feature until it provides enough value to release to production. [191]

Brian Marick[192], and later Lisa Crispin and Janet Gregory in their book "Agile Testing: A Practical Guide for Testers and Agile Teams" [193], popularized the concept of Agile Testing Quadrants, introducing a taxonomy to help teams identify and plan the testing needed. After reading a very good paper, Testing Strategies in an Agile Context[194] by Zornitsa Nikolova, I come up with a reintepretation of the original quadrant.

---

[191]https://en.wikipedia.org/wiki/Agile_testing
[192]http://www.exampler.com/old-blog/2003/08/22/#agile-testing-project-2
[193]https://www.goodreads.com/book/show/5341009-agile-testing
[194]https://www.researchgate.net/publication/337401160_Testing_Strategies_in_an_Agile_Context

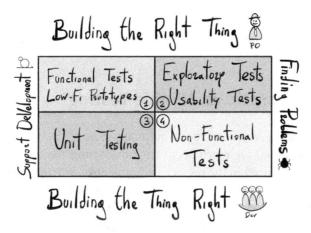

On the upper half, quadrants one and two, there are tests that try to cover Product Owners' concerns: are we building the right features? Is it going to be the product that users and stakeholders will love and use?

On the lower half, quadrants three and four, there are the tests that try to maintain good technical quality and technical debt under control, that is the main Developers' concern.

The left half, quadrants one and three, is about supporting the development cycle while the right side, quadrants two and four, is about product quality and finding problems.

- Quadrant **one** covers tests like Functional Tests, Story Tests, Prototypes and Simulation.
- Quadrant **two** covers what we call Exploratory Testing, Usability Testing, User Acceptance Testing, Alpha/Beta Testing.
- Quadrant **three** covers unit testing, and TDD.
- Quadrant **four** includes Performance and Load Testing, Security Testing and everything else, often associated with the acronym FURPS[195]

While this guidance on the type of testing may be helpful for some,

---

[195]https://en.wikipedia.org/wiki/FURPS

I don't see how just listing the type of tests could solve the problems described at the beginning of this chapter. We need something more.

## Bureaucratic vs. Nimble Testing

Coaching an AI team, I found out that people with education from the traditional approach spent time discussing the different tests they would need in the project, such as smoke test, integration test, non-regression test, etc. And, as a solution, they started writing a detail document with the differences between the different kinds of tests. Then they intended to ask their client which of the tests were required.

I pointed out that discussing the taxonomy was like when somebody points to the moon and you look at the finger. The taxonomy wasn't making the point to the question: "Are we going to test the right thing?" I then reminded the enemy of testing: False Positive and False Negative.

- **False Positive** is when the **Test Fails** while the **System Works.**
- **False Negative** is when the **Test Works** while the **System Fails.**

So I suggested the following diagram to help them to reflect on which automated test they should implement.

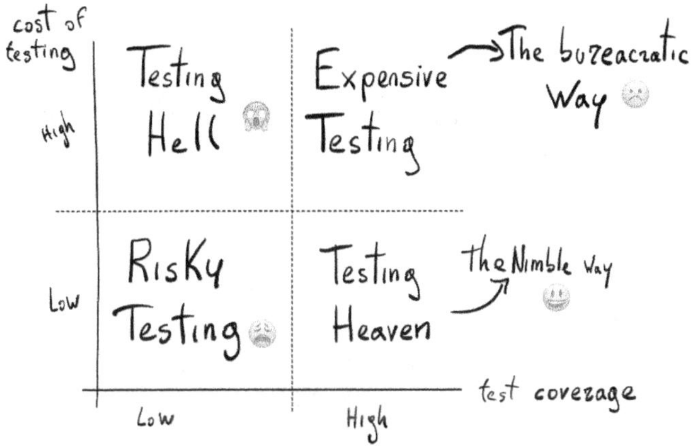

In the diagram, I compared the "Cost of Testing" with the "Test Coverage." Investing little effort on Tests with a resulting low Coverage would put them on the Risky Approach. With the technical dept increase, it will result in inevitable troubles. Investing a lot of time on documents and unnecessary bureaucracy will increase testing costs without increasing the coverage. That's what I defined Testing Hell. Traditional approaches require extensive documentation, making testing expensive. Not the best place where to be. How could we enter the Testing Heaven? We brainstormed about what increases the cost of testing without increasing the test coverage. We listed:

- Manual operations
- Slow executable tests
- Detailed documentation
- Testing the implementation of the code rather than testing the behavior
- Testing rarely used features
- Testing minor details (tooltips, labels, etc.)

## Why Most Unit Testing is Waste

James Coplien, the author of the Scrum Patterns books, described previously, published a fascinating article, titled "Why Most Unit Testing is Waste[196]," where he covers deeply the ideas about what increase the cost of testing without increasing the coverage, previously listed, and even more.

One brilliant point is that some organizations and managers often value code coverage over quality, often for reasons unrelated to quality like contracts, lack of trust, etc. The abundance of unit tests follows only the idea of reaching a specific KPI, i.e., 80% of code coverage. This requirement would become hard with ample functions, and developers find a way to solve this problem by splitting the code into smaller chunks. But James Coplien points out that:

> "If you find your testers splitting up functions to support the testing process, you're destroying your system architecture and code comprehension along with it. Test at a coarser level of granularity. (...) A smarter approach would reduce the test code mass through formal test design: that is, to do formal boundary-condition checking, more white-box testing, and so forth. That requires that the unit under test be designed for testability. This is how hardware engineers do it: designers provide "test points" that can read out values on a J-Tag pin of a chip, to access internal signal values..."

---

[196]https://rbcs-us.com/resources/articles/why-most-unit-testing-is-waste/

# Prioritizing Test by Business Risk

James Coplien, in his article "Why Most Unit Testing is Waste[197]," continues with an aspect that I believe is key in this topic:

> Tests should be designed with great care. Business people, rather than programmers, should design most functional tests. (...) In most businesses, the only tests that have business value are those that are derived from business requirements. Most unit tests are derived from programmers' fantasies about how the function should work: their hopes, stereotypes, or sometimes wishes about how things should go. Those have no provable value. (...) If this test fails, what business requirement is compromised? Most of the time, the answer is, "I don't know." If you don't know the value of the test, then the test theoretically could have zero business value. On the other hand, the test does have a cost: maintenance, computing time, administration, and so forth. That means the automated test could have a net negative value. (...) This might be the reason why Jeff Sutherland says that the PO should conceive (and at best design) the system tests as an input to, or during, Sprint Planning.

Multiple pieces of research, like the Standish Group work[198], show that the usage of the features of software follows the Pareto Ratio[199]: 20% of the features of a product represent 80% of the business value. In addition, I found in the book "Enterprise Continuous Testing[200]" an idea, in line with James Coplien's perspective, of estimating the Business Risk of each Product Backlog Item to decide

---

[197]https://rbcs-us.com/resources/articles/why-most-unit-testing-is-waste/
[198]https://www.standishgroup.com/sample_research_files/Modernization.pdf
[199]https://en.wikipedia.org/wiki/Pareto_principle
[200]https://www.tricentis.com/enterprise-continuous-testing-book/

what automate test to build. Business Risk can be formulated by estimating the frequency of the usage of features and the damage that this will create when it fails separately — then prioritizing the Automated test development with this criteria to implement only the High Business Risk Automated Test.

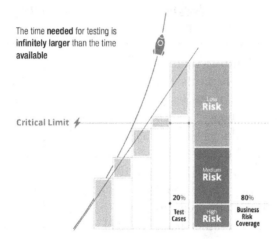

This approach would allow for prioritizing Product Backlog Items about automated testing with the same criteria as the items about features. At the same time, I consider it advisable to implement the automated test and the relative feature in the same Sprint, if possible.

## Testing with AI

Multiple authors began to introduce the topic that testing continuously will soon not be enough. The article "AI in Testing: The third wave of automation[201]" proposes the concept of Autonomous Testing with Machine Learning and AI.

> If we analyze the journey since agile came into the picture, it has completely changed the way applications

---

are delivered. Before Agile, there used to be a release in a month or sometimes more than a month. With Agile, companies are aligned to have a two-week sprint and make a release in two weeks. Continuous Testing came into the picture where automation suits were developed for regression and sanity testing to meet this. This supported quick deliveries and fast-paced testing cycles.

Now, as the world is moving towards digital transformation, the pressure to anticipate market requirements and build a system that is predictive and scalable enough to cater to future trends, going beyond continuous testing, is inevitable. Testing will need additional assistance to accelerate the process. AI, imitating intelligent human behavior for machine learning and predictive analytics, can help us get there.

EVOLUTION OF TESTING

Wolfgang Platz, in his book "Enterprise Continuous Testing[202]," expresses the same opinion: We can use AI to move Beyond Continuous Testing with the idea of "Test Smarter, Not Harder."

[202]https://www.tricentis.com/enterprise-continuous-testing-book/

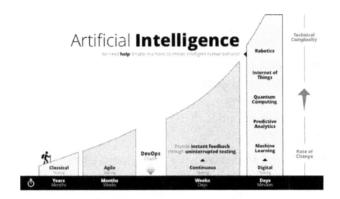

# Testing of AI

Rik Marselis in the paper Testing in the Digital Age[203] covers the topic of how to test Artificial Intelligence applications.

He says that the quality approach for a machine intelligence solution must address the following six angles:

- Mechanical
- Electrical
- Information Processing
- Machine Intelligence
- Business Impact
- Social Impact

In his article, released under the terms of Creative Common, he covers well all the above aspects, so I will not reproduce them here. He concludes his paper with a warning that is worth mentioning, though: **Beware of Testing AI with AI**

---

[203]https://www.researchgate.net/publication/337400893_Testing_in_the_Digital_Age

A special case is using artificial intelligence to test other artificial intelligence. In some cases, this may be a very appealing possibility. And however valid this option may be, before deciding to do so, the people involved must very carefully weigh the fact that they will be testing a system of which they don't exactly know what it does, by using another system of which they don't exactly know what it does. Because, all in all, this is piling up uncertainties. On the other hand, you may argue that in our modern systems of systems we have long ago become used to trusting systems we don't fully understand.

## Further Readings

- Agile Testing: A Practical Guide for Testers and Agile Teams[204] - Lisa Crispin, Janet Gregory
- Why Most Unit Testing is Waste[205] - James O Coplien
- The Future of Software Quality Assurance[206] - Stephan Goericke
- Enterprise Continuous Testing[207] - Wolfgang Platz

---

[204]https://www.goodreads.com/book/show/5341009-agile-testing
[205]https://rbcs-us.com/resources/articles/why-most-unit-testing-is-waste/
[206]https://link.springer.com/book/10.1007/978-3-030-29509-7
[207]https://www.tricentis.com/enterprise-continuous-testing-book/

# Project Chartering

**As the** Author
**I want** to introduce Liftoff
**So that** the reader understands the importance of Agile Project Charting

At the beginning of a new project it's crucial to start with right feet doing a collaborative Project Chartering. The book "Liftoff - Start and Sustain Successful Agile Teams" by Diana Larsen and Ainsley Nies describe the Liftoff concept for project chartering that I think is really appropriated for complex projects like Artificial Intelligence.

## Liftoff

For Agile Project Chartering we mean a high-level summary of the key success factors of the project, typically elaborated in the form of information radiators, like posters for co-located teams, or virtual boards like miro.com[208] or mural.co[209], for remote teams. According to the Agile Chartering model of the Liftoff book, there are three phases to complete: *Purpose, Alignment, Context.*

## Purpose

*Purpose* is the reason why a project is carried out; the activity with this name offers support and inspiration in trying to understand what drives us to create a given product.

---

[208]http://miro.com
[209]http://mural.co

## The definition of Value

## Basic Canvas

To facilitate the brainstorming of the vision and the value of a project, I developed The Basic Canvas, a variation of Roman Pichler's Product Vision Board[210] that I released under a Creative Commons license and freely downloadable from my personal website[211].

| The Basic Canvas | Project: | | Date: |
|---|---|---|---|
| Who is it for? | Needs and Desire | Solution | Expectation |
| Who is not for? | Obstacles | Alternatives | Risks |

Basic Canvas

It discusses who our customers are and which aren't their needs, desires, and the obstacles they encounter in trying to reach them. In my opinion, this scenario is the basic definition of value, and it is represented in the left half of the Canvas. When someone has an impediment to satisfying his desire, they are willing to exchange value with somebody who can help him in his goal. The right half of the Canvas, therefore, allows us to discuss what we can offer

---

[210]https://www.romanpichler.com/tools/product-vision-board/
[211]https://paolo.sammiche.li/download

to help those listed on the left side achieve their goals and what are the alternatives to our idea today. The last column captures the Business expectations from the Sponsors of the initiative and the risks in satisfying these ambitions.

To develop the Basic Canvas, I normally divide the participants into different tables, in which different canvases were created in parallel. Then, in a large wall, we combined the ideas that emerged at each table into final artifact that remains for the project's duration.

## Alignment

The Alignment phase has the objective to create the alliance that leads to the result described in the Purpose phase. To create an alliance, the objective of the initiative must be aligned with the personal objectives of the people who take part into it. We all win if we win together; or, as stated in the slogan of the Liftoff book, "Came As Individuals, Left As a Team".

The activities envisaged in the Alignment are the identification of the core teams, if necessary, the definition of working agreements and the definition of values.

In Scrum, there are several Working Agreements:

- The Working Agreement, understood as the set of simple rules that govern the life of the team.
- The Definition of Done, a set of criteria that must be respected to consider a job as complete.
- The Definition of Ready, a criterion that establishes when the items of a Product Backlog are sufficiently clear to be eligible for Sprint Planning.

The last described activity is that of identifying team values.

Some teams adopt Scrum values: Respect, Courage, Commitment, Openness and Focus; others prefer to choose their own. It depends a lot on the context: my advice as a coach is to leave the team in full autonomy.

## Context

No man is an island... let alone a team in a company.
It is necessary to identify how the nascent initiative is placed in the company context and which interactions it must have with the Single Matter Experts, with the Stakeholders and with other teams. To do this, it is useful to create a chart that illustrates the relationships.

Other activities of this last phase are the identification and discussion of available resources (time, external media, budget, workspaces, suppliers and equipment, tools, training, etc.). Another fundamental aspect is the discussion of the product's starting architecture, its modules and interfaces: these are the basis of an Agile Architecture. To finish, it is necessary to proceed to a risk analysis activity, for example listing a FUD backlog[212] and then categorizing the items one by one in a ROAM scheme: Resolved, Owned, Accepted, Mitigated[213].

The final activity consists in the creation of the initial Product Backlog using one of the different methods described in the next chapter.

# Further readings

- Liftoff: Launching Agile Teams & Projects[214] - Diana Larsen, Ainsley Nies

---

[212]Fear, Uncertainty and Doubts
[213]Resolved, Owned, Accepted, Mitigated. Each activity is discussed and classified in one of these four categories.
[214]https://www.goodreads.com/book/show/13493815-liftoff

# Product Backlog Creation

**As the** Author
**I want** to describe the different methods to populate an initial Product Backlog
**So that** the reader understands the different approaches and find the one more suitable for their project

## Impact Mapping

Impact Mapping is a Product Backlog elicitation technique by Gojko Adzic, published in 2014 in his book "Impact Mapping Making a big impact with software products and projects[215]." Gojco says that Impact mapping is a variant of the InUse effect mapping method[216], introduced by Mijo Balic and Ingrid Domingues (Ottersten), combined with:

- Impact Maps for training organizations[217] invented by Robert O. Brinkerhoff
- The Feature Injection ideas[218] of Chris Matts
- The Measurability and Iterative Delivery ideas[219] of Tom Gilb[220].

---

[215]https://www.goodreads.com/book/show/16084015-impact-mapping
[216]https://www.inuse.se/read/birth-impact-mapping/
[217]https://www.innovativelg.com/user_area/content_media/raw/Impact_Mapping_WhitePaper_Final.pdf
[218]https://www.infoq.com/articles/feature-injection-success/
[219]http://concepts.gilb.com/dl792
[220]https://en.wikipedia.org/wiki/Tom_Gilb

An impact mapping is a visual tool to collaboratively share the scope and underlying assumptions between technical and business people. It is a Mind Map[221] created during a discussion facilitated by answering the following four questions:

1. Why?
2. Who?
3. How?
4. What?

The following image shows an example from the Open Source Workshop Material[222] published by the Author.

---
[221]https://en.wikipedia.org/wiki/Mind_map
[222]https://github.com/impactmapping/open-impact-mapping-workshop

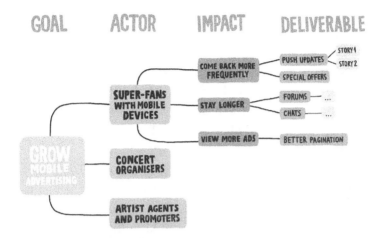

I was inspired to try this approach after listening to Gojco explaining it during the keynote of the Italian Agile Day 2016 "Impact Mapping with Innovation Games[223]." I highly recommend watching this video. It's informative and, at some traits, funny.

## AI Impact Mapping

When I found myself using this technique with AI Development, I needed some adjustments, though. Gojco crafted the approach with User-Centered Design in mind. Not all software development is about user-centered products, meaning that the interaction with the user is not the central part, so in that situation, you need to change the approach. That was the case of a Bank that asked me to coach their Team, developing a new Credit Score algorithm using Machine Learning. The interaction of the product consisted of a Bank employee pressing a button and getting a number. This number will hint if and how much to grant to the client in terms of credit. The interactive part, the data gathering from the user, the visualization, etc., was not part of the project's scope, and it was mainly in place already. The goal was to build a better algorithm made outdated by the COVID-19 changes in the landscape.

[223]https://gojko.net/2016/12/15/impact-mapping-iad.html

When I started learning about AI Development, many experts repeated the same Mantra: "start with the Data." Artificial Intelligence
development, for the algorithm development part at least, sounds
more like a Data-Centered Design rather than a User-Centered
Design. It is not that the human being doesn't appear in the
scenario, it was the causation of the data in our case, but the critical
part was the data we could use, not the people's interaction with
the product.

To introduce Impact Mapping to Management, I used the metaphor
of Google Maps, the same that Gojco uses in his talk.

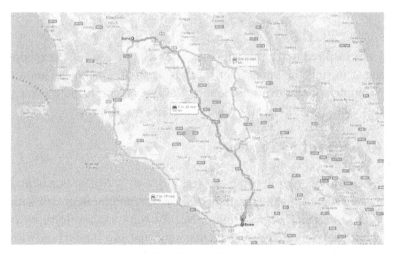

**Google Maps routes from Siena to Rome, Italy. ©2021 Google**

I said, "if I want to go from my home town Siena to Rome,
Google Maps shows me alternative routes. One highlight is the
best one, given the current situation, and all the possible routes are
labeled with the distance, in my case in kilometers, and the average
time. That is a roadmap! The one you should use for software
development. The roadmaps you normally see on the presentations
of a new project are "a road," not a roadmap because they do not
contain alternatives. But also, this roadmap does not mean that I
will go through all the roads. When I reach my destination with

success, it doesn't matter which route I used.

We're going to use an Agile Process Framework called Scrum to develop our project. It works just like Google Maps Navigator[224] and Waze[225]: it will check the traffic ahead constantly and recalculate the optimal path if needed."

So we showed them the impact mapping I helped the Scrum Team to draft.

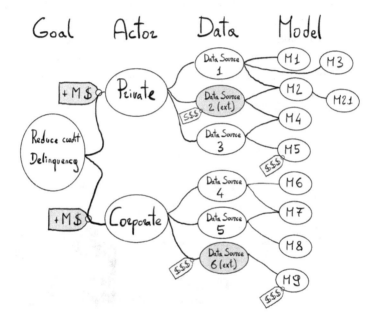

In this diagram, we show the **Why**, the goal of the project, the **Who**, the Actors involved in the analysis, the **What** we know, the data we have, or we can acquire, and the **How**, the Model we could use to generate the insights.

The project Goal is to Reduce Credit Delinquency. We have two main actors: Private and Corporate clients. They are a rough categorization that we will refine later. For example, we can divide the

---

[224]https://play.google.com/store/apps/details?id=com.google.android.apps.maps
[225]https://play.google.com/store/apps/details?id=com.waze

Corporate Clients across the different industries starting from the data on how COVID-19 affected the various sectors. We attached "price tags" in the Impact Mapping. If they show a plus and are green, it means that is money the bank can save. If they are yellow, they tell the rough estimation of additional costs, like acquiring external data or buying expert models from consultancy firms.

So I let the Scrum Team explain the map, add ideas from the participants and add notes and clarification on top of the Mind-Map. The workshop ended by agreeing on a single path to create the first version. To make the Management understand the real meaning of Iterative and Incremental Development, I used the picture from Gojco's book Impact Mapping, and I invited them to attend the Sprint Reviews:

# Seven Dimensions

In the case of user-centric development, the "7 Dimension" technique, described in the Discovery to Deliver[226] book by Ellen Gottesdiener and Mary Gorman, would be a good choice. I learned

---

[226]https://www.discovertodeliver.com

this technique from Scrum Inc's Product Owner class, so even Jeff Sutherland recommends it. The Seven Dimensions are used to facilitate the conversation with the stakeholders in a workshop, in my case, the final part of the LiftOff, but it could also be used to further slicing a User Story during a Product Backlog Refinement.

Some dimensions (USER, ACTION, DATA, and CONTROL) are about Functional Requirements: they define specific behaviors, actions, or interactions with the system. The remaining ones (IN-TERFACE, ENVIRONMENT, and QUALITY) are Nonfunctional Requirements, meaning that they define the criteria and characteristics of the system. The visual tool aims to guide through questions that help elicit the requirements and needs from a user point of view. Let's see the dimensions with the related questions I use to facilitate the conversation during the workshop.

## User

What are the users that will interact with the Product? What is their background? What is the goal they want to achieve? Another technique I sometimes use in combination with this section is the User Persona[227].

## Interface

What are the interfaces that will connect the users with the system? This dimension may have a relationship with the environment where the user will access the Product. Is it going to be an office application only? Is it also Mobile? Or maybe it's not even an

---

[227]https://en.wikipedia.org/wiki/Persona_(user_experience)

application: the user wants only to be notified by email with a weekly report.

## Action

What Actions will be required from the users to provide the needed capabilities? Is there a specific workflow? How is an action triggered? How does the Product respond? How do actions impact Data?

## Data

What source of Data will be involved to provide the highlighted capability? How often do we need to update it? Who could help to annotate it? How do you know whether the Data is valid or not?

## Control

What are the Controls we need to perform? What are the risks if the Product does not comply with the control needs? Is there any limitation and privacy/security concerns with the Data?

## Environment

What are the physical properties and the technological platforms involved? Where will the user be when using our application? On which kind of device?

## Quality Attribute

What are the quality attributes? Many of the FURPS[228] quality attributes apply, like Functionality, Usability, Reliability, Performance, Security, and others.

---

[228]https://en.wikipedia.org/wiki/FURPS

As we noticed, the Product Dimensions focus on one aspect of the Product, so they depend on other Dimensions. The book shows a Canvas to highlight these relationships.

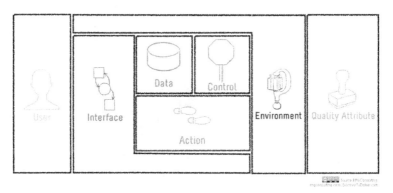

Coaching a Scrum@Scale setting with multiple NLP Scrum Team working together, I was facing the challenge to facilitate the LiftOff with an unusual business scenario: the Product we were about to build would serve four different Use Case from four very different types of users, some of them very technical, other with a scientific background, and others business and market-oriented. So I decided to use the 7 Dimensions technique to highlight the differences of the various use cases. First, we brainstormed all these Dimensions for all the use cases involved (it required one workshop for each case since the stakeholders were different). Then highlighting the high-level elements in common between all the use cases, we forged the first set of user stories to build the MVP[229].

---

[229]https://en.wikipedia.org/wiki/Minimum_viable_product

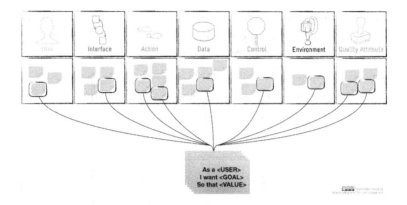

The USER and ACTION dimensions help draft the User Story, which stays on the front of the card, together with the VALUE statement. The remaining dimensions are used to create the Acceptance Criteria, traditionally on the back of the card. Section 3 of the book Discovery to Deliver, freely downloadable from their website[230], contains a detailed description of each dimension.

# User Story Mapping

User Story Mapping[231] is a brainstorming technique invented and popularized by Jeff Patton[232]. It organizes the different features on a bidimensional map that supports a rich conversation with stakeholders and allows grouping features in releases.

If I have a significant part of the audience that never worked with this practice, I start with the following warm-up [233].

---

[230]https://www.discovertodeliver.com/download.php

[231]https://www.jpattonassociates.com/story-mapping/

[232]https://www.jpattonassociates.com/about-jeff-patton-associates/

[233]Images from Aaron Sanders slides https://www.slideshare.net/aaronsanders/passionate-product-ownership Creative Commons BY-NC-SA

I ask some participants to write sticky notes with their actions from the moment they woke up to when they got into the office (or online, if remote working), one thing per sticky note. Then we arrange the sticky notes horizontally, in chronological order, on a large wall, and combine actions from the different participants, removing duplicates. The order doesn't need to be strictly chronological; some people do breakfast and then shower, and others do vice versa. This way, we get a list of items in a plausible chronological order. At that point, we create clusters putting a label over it, like "food," "personal hygiene," clothing, etc., getting something like the following picture:

Then I pick up a participant, and I ask a question: "Imagine you wake up one hour late; what action would you do anyway, move them down one row." In this way, we get the essential items under the commonly performed items. "Now, imagine you wake up with the sound of the fire alarm; what action would you do anyway, move them down one row more." At that point, we get three lists: actions usually done, activities done even when late, and essential activities. I use these two questions to show participants that prioritization is always possible and how to identify different releases by vertically arranging the activities.

Finally, we can start brainstorming the feature of the real product. The main backbone comprises user tasks that represent the user's journey through the product, so we start from that. Depending on the grain size of the user tasks you identify during the brainstorming, you can group them and add a label, like in the ice break exercise, or split them into activities, if they are gross grained. Some people found it helpful to identify these different grains with Epic, Feature, and Story. I usually don't stress the terminology too much since other books use it differently (for some authors, Epic is bigger than a Feature, for others is vice versa). In the end, you will have a bidimensional map of user actions, representing the features of your product. In the following picture, the example of an email client from the Registered Product Owner[234] class by Scrum Inc.

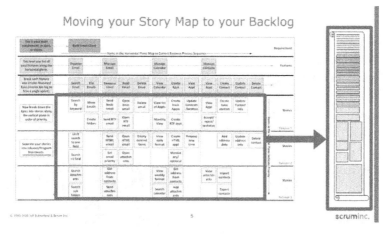

With the User Story Mapping, you can build your Product Backlog, where the ordering of the story is by priority. Many product owners maintain the user story mapping to keep reflecting on the different

---

[234]https://agileeducation.org/scrum-product-owner/

features since it's not convenient to reflect on new features directly on the priority ordered list you have in the Product Backlog. Some Agile Tools allow maintaining the two views synchronized, which is helpful to monitor development; for this regard, Jeff Patton recommends in his material tagging stories to show progress[235].

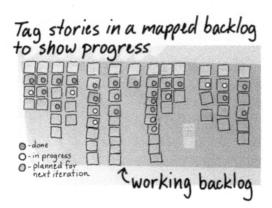

## Further readings

- Impact Mapping: Making a Big Impact with Software Products and Projects[236] - Gojko Adzic
- User Story Mapping: Discover the Whole Story, Build the Right Product[237] - Jeff Patton, Peter Economy
- Specification by Example[238] - Gojko Adzic
- Discovery to Delivery[239] - Ellen Gottesdiener, Mary Gorman

---

[235]Image from Jeff Patton "Passionate Product Leadership" handouts https://www.jpattonassociates.com/handouts/ Creative Commons BY-NC-SA

[236]https://www.goodreads.com/book/show/16084015-impact-mapping

[237]https://www.goodreads.com/book/show/22221112-user-story-mapping

[238]https://www.goodreads.com/book/show/10288718-specification-by-example

[239]https://www.discovertodeliver.com/download.php

# Multiple Teams

**As the** Author
**I want** to describe the topic of Scaling Scrum
**So that** the reader understands how to build complex products with multiple teams.

## Challenges to Scaling

When you need to scale up, from a single Scrum Team to an organization of multiple teams and dozens or hundreds of people, you have to consider numerous constraints. One first critical constrain is the relationship between the organization and the product architecture, as defined by Conway's Law.

### Conway's Law

Conway's law states that organizations will create systems that reflect their communication structure. Melvin Conway, a computer scientist, proposed this concept in 1967. His original phrase was as follows:

> Any organization that designs a system will produce a design whose structure is a copy of the organization's communication structure.

A Massachusetts Institute of Technology (MIT) Team and Harvard Business School researchers published evidence supporting Conway's law. They claimed that the "product developed by the loosely-coupled organization is significantly more modular than the product developed by the tightly-coupled organization," using "the mirroring hypothesis" as an equivalent term for Conway's law. The authors emphasize the significance of "organizational design decisions on the technical structure of the objects that these organizations generate afterward." [240]

Eric S. Raymond[241], one of the fathers of Open Source Movement[242], in the book "The Cathedral and the Bazaar[243]" describe the same concept as follows:

> If you have four groups working on a compiler, you'll get a 4-pass compiler

## Elon Musk on Agile Architecture

I found an excellent explanation of Conway's Law and an incredibly inspiring introduction to the Agile Architecture principles in the "A conversation with Elon Musk about Starship[244]" interview from the Everyday Astronaut[245] youtube channel.

---

[240]https://en.wikipedia.org/wiki/Conway%27s_law#Supporting_evidence
[241]https://en.wikipedia.org/wiki/Eric_S._Raymond
[242]https://en.wikipedia.org/wiki/Open_source
[243]https://en.wikipedia.org/wiki/The_Cathedral_and_the_Bazaar
[244]https://www.youtube.com/watch?v=cIQ36Kt7UVg
[245]https://www.youtube.com/channel/UC6uKrU_WqJ1R2HMTY3LIx5Q

Following an adapted transcript of the significant parts of Elon Musk's perspective, divided by topics:

## Simple Design

I think I've learned a lot of lessons about how to make things go fast. And then I've propagated those lessons to the SpaceX team, and there's just like an incredibly talented, hard-working team at SpaceX. We have taken the general approach of "**if a design is taking too long, the design is wrong**," and therefore, the design must be modified to accelerate progress. And one of the most fundamental errors made in advanced developments is to stick to a design, even when it is very complicated, and not strive to delete parts and processes.

## Who's the Chief Engineer?

I was actually at dinner with a friend, and he was like, "Well, who's the chief engineer at SpaceX?" - Oh, I go, "It's me," "No, no," he's like, "It's not you, who is it?", "Okay, it's either someone with a very low ego or, I don't know." You know, what I actually used to tell the team is: "**Everyone is a Chief Engineer.**" This is extremely important, that everyone must understand how, broadly speaking, all the systems in the vehicle work.

## The Conway's Law

And so that you don't have self-system optimization, because this is naturally what happens, you can see "**the product errors reflect the organizational errors.**" So like essentially, you'll see that there's an interface at this particular, like, whatever departments you've got, that will be where your interfaces are. Instead of getting rid of something or questioning the constraints, the one department will design to the constraints that the other department has given them without calling into question those constraints and saying, "Those constraints are wrong." You should actually take the approach that the constraints you are given are guaranteed to be some degree wrong because the counterpoint would be that they are perfect, which is never.

## Perfection doesn't exist

As you were saying like, what's the probability that this is a platonic ideal of a perfect part? Zero, okay, so question your constraints. It does not matter if the person handing you those constraints won a Nobel Prize. Even our own standards are wrong some of the time. So, question your constraints; this is extremely important. Another thing is, "What are the mistakes that smart engineers make?" **One of the biggest traps for smart engineers is optimizing something that shouldn't exist.**

### Questions more than Answers

When you go through college, and you're like studying physics or engineering, I studied physics, you have to answer the question that the professor gives you, you don't get to say, "This is the wrong question." But, in reality, we have far more degrees. When you're in reality, you have all the degrees of freedom of reality, and so the first thing you should say is, "This question is wrong." It took ages to frame the question. I mean, it's just like "The Hitchhiker's Guide to the Galaxy," Douglas Adams, I think, best philosophy book ever. His book is so deep that people don't even understand. But like, in The Hitchhiker's Guide to the Galaxy, the Earth is a giant computer, and it comes up with the answer "42" to the question "what's the answer to life, the universe, and everything?" The answer's 42, and they're like, "What the hell, that doesn't make any sense." So **the really hard part is the question, the answer is the easy part**, you need a much more powerful computer to tell you what the question is, and this is true, at the point in which you can properly frame the question, the answer is comparatively easy.

# Agile Architecture principles

Given Conway's Law, it is conceptually wrong to evaluate an organizational architecture without having the product architecture on the side and vice-versa. The two will influence each other, and the strongest will drive the other. Since the purpose of any company is to deliver friction-less value to customers, the organization should be the simplest human structure to deliver value through a product. Let's see some Product Architecture principles on Agile terms.

# What is an Agile Architecture

If we go back to Alistair Cockburn definition of Agile "the ability to move and change direction, quickly and with ease," an Agile Architecture is the one who makes it easy to change and improve the product or, like Craig Larman[246] often repeat, "to turn on a dime for a dime." This means that *Design for Change* is more important than design for perfection at the first strike.

So, if the architecture is fully emergent, in some way evolutionary, this means that you shouldn't take any up-front design decision? The truth is that Architecture, in Agile terms, is *"the set of all the decisions that you cannot not take."* You will always have some decisions to make upfront.

# Modularity

The typical Agile approach is to encapsulate these design decisions that you *cannot not take* into modules. What is a module? Joe Justice, founder of the Wikispeed[247] project, helped me understand the difference between a Module and a Component. Since the product in the Wikispeed project is a fuel-efficient car, I will use this example because it is easier to be visually represented than a software architecture.

## Modules vs Components

Let's define the module of a product as a means to deliver value perceived by the customer. A component, instead, would be a convenient way to separate elements, given their technical nature. An easy example of this concept is Wikispeed architecture.

---

[246]https://en.wikipedia.org/wiki/Craig_Larman
[247]https://en.wikipedia.org/wiki/Wikispeed

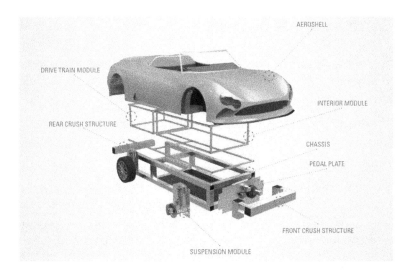

The aeroshell, for example, is a module because it serves all the requirements of aesthetics and aerodynamics. Likewise, the suspension serves all the stability, comfort, and safety needs. On the other hand, the breaks are a component because they alone are not entirely responsible for user requirements.

The principle is to have Product Backlog Items impacting one or as few as possible modules. This enables teams to work on different modules during the same Sprint without interfering with each other.

Identifying all the product modules would be challenging initially because this means knowing all the product requirements and crafting a clear Product Backlog in advance.

Joe Justice suggests starting with the simplest possible design and then giving it to a Scrum Team and letting them iterate and evolve the architecture. This suggestion perfectly matches Elon Musk's interview's "Simple Design" Principe.

## Contract First Design

So, let's pretend you have a speculative design of the modules of your product. What you do then is to start building one module after the other, right? Well, not exactly.

The first step would be to build the scaffold of every module starting from the interfaces. This approach is called "Contract First Design."

Contract First Design means defining the interface between modules and building the simplest form of the module, starting from the interface. It's vital to coach the Developers to allow space for growth in the interface, anticipate possible evolutions, and create a "decoupling strategy" to develop any module independently (See Dependencies First[248] Pattern).

When somebody working on a Module recognizes the need to change the interface, the process is to "Stop the Line[249]," collect all the people involved around the interface, agree on a new interface, implement the change, and then get back to work.

My perspective is that the Contract First Design is not something that you **build on the product**, but is more a *process* to define and update the agreements between modules as soon as this is needed.

While I was reflecting on this topic to write this chapter, somebody on my Linkedin network posted: "Coupling is highly problematic. This applies to teams even more than code."

James Coplien[250] commented in a way that caught my attention: "This is a common naive generalization and simplification. Essential coupling is what builds relationship. Accidental coupling only gets in the way. The goal is not to reduce coupling. The goal is to reduce accidental coupling while leveraging essential coupling to your advantage."

---

[248]http://scrumbook.org/value-stream/sprint-backlog/dependencies-first.html
[249]https://en.wikipedia.org/wiki/Andon_(manufacturing)
[250]https://en.wikipedia.org/wiki/Jim_Coplien

Focussing on the essential coupling while reducing the unneeded coupling is a fascinating principle.

With a **Loosely Coupled Product Architecture**, companies can reduce time-to-market and upgrade their product to maintain them future-proof. Lastly, this enables a loosely coupled relationship with the organizational structure if you leverage the other significant constraint of scaling the product organization: Skillsets.

## Skills and Teams

With a modularized product, you can theoretically develop them in parallel, reducing the time-to-market dramatically. A simplistic approach would be to assign one team for each Module and hope not to get oversized Product Backlog Items where heavy development affects multiple modules.

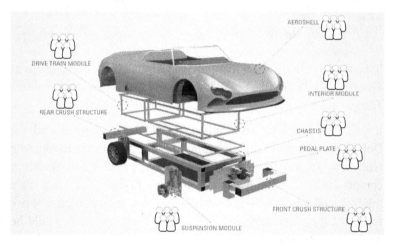

But with an organization like this, how could they "question the constraints" given by the other teams?

The approach would be the same we use with an individual to develop compencies but for the entire team. Every team should self assess the ability to work in each Module with the same three levels:

- Junior - we can work on the Module, but with somebody mentoring us
- Senior - we can work on the Module
- Master - somebody of us can mentor another team on this Module

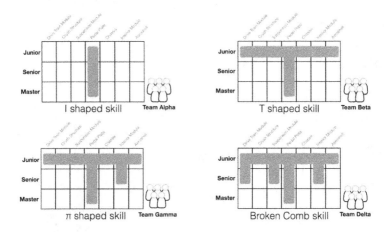

In Large Scale Scrum[251], a team like the Alpha is called "Component Team" while Teams like Beta, Gamma, and Delta are called Features Teams.

It will be critical to have only teams like the Gamma and the Delta to scale up the organization and maintain innovation and a really evolutionary approach to the product architecture. However, compositions like Team Alpha would be problematic since they might become a bottleneck or remain without enough high-priority work. At the same time, something like the Team Beta would be acceptable as a transitioning to the "π Shaped Skill."

Skillset is the ultimate constraint when you design organizations. Learning a new skill takes time, and people have preferences and different attitudes, so it's a long, slow and difficult process. Therefore, it's critical to highlight the bottlenecks in terms of skillset and

---

[251]https://less.works/less/structure/feature-teams

to implement all the possible measures to enable the organization to keep learning continuously.

# Recommended Patterns & Practices

The first consideration is to scale only when you absolutely need it; a single Scrum Team working on the entire product would be the best option for the most. This quote from the paragraph Scaling Sequence[252] from the Scrum Pattern Books[253] recap the essence of this concept.

> Scaling is not about transforming an existing micro-managed organization to an Agile one. When someone asks, "We have over 500 developers: how do we scale to Scrum?" is an example of someone asking the wrong question. How do they know they need 500 developers? Nor is "scaling" a proper response to a product that is late in delivery. Brook's Law[254] —that adding people to a late project makes it later— still applies at team level. Scaling is about the piecemeal growth of the Development Teams in response to the growth of the product itself. Scrum has always scaled in that sense. Jeff Sutherland started the first multi-team Scrum at IDX in 1994. Exactly how Scrum scales is in large part situational, but the following patterns are common.

## Mitosis

> One should grow a Scrum Team in an incremental, piecemeal fashion, but eventually the team just becomes too large to remain efficient

---

[252]http://scrumbook.org/product-organization-pattern-language/a-scaling-sequence.html
[253]http://scrumbook.org
[254]https://en.wikipedia.org/wiki/Brooks%27s_law

Therefore

Differentiate a single large Development Team into two
small teams after it gradually grows to the point of
inefficiency—about seven people in the old team.[255]

The idea of the Mitosis pattern is to use the biological approach of
splitting a development team in two while adding new people to
the new teams. In this way, there will always be somebody from
the original team within the new team, and with new people, they
will become high-performing and capable of working on the entire
product over time.

According to Jeff Sutherland, the ideal number of a Scrum team
is five. This number comes from a study [256] showing the perfect
number to be an average of 4.6 members[257], so as soon as you exceed
the number six, you should start splitting the team[258], eventually
adding new members to maintain the team cross-functionality.

Initial
Team

Mitosis
(Team Splitting)

Mitosis
(Team Splitting)

In this example, we move from a team of six developers to an
organization of 24 people with two mitoses. The benefit of this
approach is that in each team after the second mitosis, at least
one person is from the original team of six, which maintains the
memory of decisions made in the initial design.

How long to maintain a team intact before splitting? Starting from
the notion from Cognitive science that to form a new habit takes 21

---

[255]http://scrumbook.org/product-organization-pattern-language/mitosis.html
[256]Hackman & Vidmar (1970). Effects of Size and Task Type on Group Performance and
Member Reactions. Sociometry. https://doi.org/10.2307/2786271
[257]https://money.cnn.com/magazines/fortune/fortune_archive/2006/06/12/8379238/
[258]https://www.scruminc.com/scrum-keep-team-size-under-7/

days[259], my observation is that a Scrum Team requires between four to eight two-weeks Sprints to establish the rituals and consolidate the Working Agreements, Definition of Done[260], etc. Therefore, I would not recommend any team change, like adding new people or splitting the teams more frequently than every six months. The Stable Teams[261] pattern shows that this process should happen only with clear business benefits in scaling up the development organization since maintaining a stable team is way more effective than adding new staffing.

## Scrum of Scrums

When multiple teams work independently of each other they tend to focus myopically on their own concerns and lose sight of any common goals.

Therefore

Give the right and the responsibility to collaborate on delivering common goals identified by the Product Owner to the Development Teams themselves. Permit the teams to figure out the best way to coordinate their efforts.[262]

The Mitosis pattern creates the need for cross-team coordination, which leads to the Scrum of Scrums pattern. This pattern is also the founding stone of the Scrum@Scale framework[263], authored by Jeff Sutherland. The critical aspect is that this pattern gives "the right and the responsibility to collaborate on delivering common goals ... to the Development Teams themselves," creating a concept that in

[259]https://jamesclear.com/new-habit
[260]http://scrumbook.org/value-stream/definition-of-done.html
[261]http://scrumbook.org/product-organization-pattern-language/development-team/stable-teams.html
[262]http://scrumbook.org/product-organization-pattern-language/scrum-of-scrums.html
[263]https://www.scrumatscale.com

Scrum@Scale is called **Team of Teams**.[264] This is the essence, in my opinion: it's not a paternalistic approach where managers organize and coordinate multiple teams, but Developers with the maturity and the duty to find the best way to coordinate the development with the Managers.

What does means *Team of Teams*? If a Team is a "group of individuals working together and helping each other reach the common goal," a *Team of Teams* is a "group of Teams working together and helping each other reach the common goal."

The need for coordination between multiple teams leads to the implementation of patterns like:

- Sprinting at the same cadence (Organizational Sprint Pulse[265]).
- Maintaining a common Definition of Done[266].
- Common Scaled Events, like Sprint Planning[267], Sprint Review[268], Product Backlog Refinement[269], and Sprint Retrospective[270].
- Scaled Daily Scrum[271], with representatives from each Team, just after the teams' Daily Scrum, to resolve emergent dependencies and issues.

To foster collaboration and maintain the ability of "Working together and helping each other" I found it beneficial to create at Sprint Planning a buffer for interruptions[272] in every Sprint Backlog,

---

[264]The concept and the term "Team of Teams" is originated in General Stanley McChrystal's book "Team of Teams: New Rules of Engagement for a Complex World": https://www.goodreads.com/book/show/22529127-team-of-teams

[265]http://scrumbook.org/product-organization-pattern-language/organizational-sprint-pulse.html

[266]http://scrumbook.org/value-stream/definition-of-done.html

[267]http://scrumbook.org/value-stream/sprint-planning.html

[268]http://scrumbook.org/value-stream/sprint-review.html

[269]http://scrumbook.org/value-stream/product-backlog/refined-product-backlog.html

[270]http://scrumbook.org/value-stream/sprint/sprint-retrospective.html

[271]http://scrumbook.org/value-stream/sprint/daily-scrum.html

[272]http://scrumbook.org/product-organization-pattern-language/illegitimus-non-interruptus.html

and perform the Emergency Procedure[273] pattern as soon as one Team encounter an issue.

With the increase of the number of teams and the maturity of the product, it will be helpful to organize a Release Plan[274] event, so that both developers and stakeholders have the visibility and the understanding of the midterm goals, maintaining the releases to production small and frequent (Responsive Deployment[275] pattern).

## Product Owner Team

The Product Owner has more to do than a single person can handle well

Therefore

Create a Product Owner Team, led by the Chief Product Owner, whose members together carry out product ownership.[276]

Artificial Intelligence is a malleable and universally applicable technology. So, while developing an application with a specific business use case in mind, I've often seen that many other use cases arise, especially in large organizations. The temptation is to maximize the return of the investment by developing general applications and using them in different contexts, trying to *kill two birds with one stone*. So you start with many use cases, different kinds of stakeholders, multiple countries and business units involved, etc. It quickly becomes too much work for a single heroic Product Owner. In this context, I found the "Product Owner Team" to be an effective pattern that increases the ability to manage the expectation of a large and diverse set of stakeholders. At the same

---

[273]http://scrumbook.org/product-organization-pattern-language/emergency-procedure.html

[274]http://scrumbook.org/value-stream/release-plan.html

[275]http://scrumbook.org/value-stream/responsive-deployment.html

[276]http://scrumbook.org/product-organization-pattern-language/product-owner-team.html

time, it maintains a single cohesive vision of the product, carried out by the Chief Product Owner. The members of the PO Team should have complementary skills, compared to the Chief Product Owner, such as Computer Science, Business Domains, Design and User Experience, and others, to increase the understanding of the vast Product Domain.

How big should a PO Team be? I would say the smallest as possible, often I've seen three as a good number, and if you ask Jeff Sutherland, he will undoubtedly say "no more than five."

To talk with the developers without ambiguity, understanding the needs and requirements from a diverse crowd of stakeholders to take the decision and directions, they will need an event of clarification that anticipates the Product Backlog Refinement[277]: the MetaScrum Pattern.

## MetaScrum

> Scrum Teams are in place, but direction (or the threat of interference) from legacy management structures causes confusion about the locus of control over product content and direction.
>
> Therefore
>
> Create a MetaScrum as a forum where the entire enterprise can align behind the Product Owners' backlogs at every level of Scrum in the organization.[278]

MetaScrum is the event that anticipates the understanding of the business needs and gets clarity for the Product Owner Team (it would also work with a single Product Owner, but in the context of AI development, I will consider the two patterns working together). MetaScrum is the place where the beliefs that will drive prioritization are formed.

---

[277]http://scrumbook.org/value-stream/product-backlog/refined-product-backlog.html
[278]http://scrumbook.org/product-organization-pattern-language/metascrum.html

Who should attend the MetaScrum? Would developers be present? What's the difference with the Product Backlog Refinement, then? In my experience, a good ratio between technical people and business people is 20/80, symmetrically between Refinement and MetaScrum, like a sort of yin and yang[279].

- MetaScrum: 80% of the participants are from business and 20% from development (usually few representatives from the team)
- Refinement: 80% of the participants are the developers and 20% from business (normally the PO Team and a few key stakeholders if necessary)

The goal of a MetaScrum is to create Product Backlog Items that are Good Enough to be discussed during a Product Backlog Refinement with the Developers. In my experience, the introduction of the MetaScrum makes two natural levels of clarity between Product Backlog Items. Therefore, I used the term *Good Enough* (or just *Good*) to differentiate these items from the *Ready* concept introduced in the Scrum Guide and detailed in the Definition of Ready[280] Pattern.

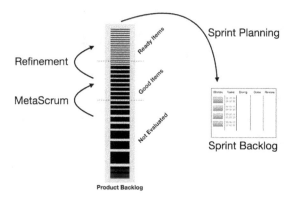

[279]https://en.wikipedia.org/wiki/Yin_and_yang
[280]http://scrumbook.org/value-stream/product-backlog/definition-of-ready.html

While coaching MetaScrum events, to facilitate the conversation, I developed some guiding questions, like:

- Which capability are we delivering now? Did we identify the 20/80 ratio of the Value?
- What capability should we deliver next?
- How will our users use the capability to generate Business Value? What are the constrains?
- Is there an opportunity for new Capabilities?

To facilitate MetaScrum events in clarifying the PBI and maintaining a high level of participation, I experimented with the following techniques (valid as well for Product Backlog Refinement).

## Triple Nichel

This approach is inspired by the Triple Nickels in Retrospectives[281]. My adaptation aims to quickly clarify the most straightforward PBI, involving everybody only for the more complex requirement.

I organized a circle of "Pods," trying to have a diverse composition. For example, with business stakeholders and two teams, I created Pods of three people with one developer from each team and one stakeholder. Depending on the context, you'll figure out; the principle is diversity, so don't create a pod of developers and a pod of business people only. The Chief Product Owner remains outside the Pods, moving from one to another when is requested.

---

[281]https://gscokart.wordpress.com/2013/02/02/triple-nickels-in-retrospectives/

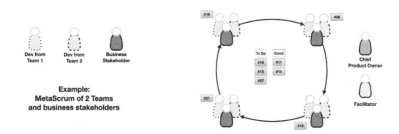

Identify the PBIs to discuss with a token (I often write the ID of the PBI from the software tool on a sticky note) and put them in the center of the table. Each pod pulls one item, reads it on the software tool, and discusses it. They ask themselves questions about the meaning of the item and collect the answers to these questions as acceptance criteria, if they know it, or as an unresolved question if they don't know it. After a time-box of 10 or 15 minutes, every pod passes the item to the next pod through the circle. If a pod considers a PBI clear enough, they mark it with a green dot. Depending on the number of pods, an item is "Good" (or Ready, if you use this technique during a Product Backlog Refinement) when it has two or three green dots. If a Pod receives an item without any green dot that has already been discussed, call the Chief Product Owner to clarify the unresolved questions. If needed, the facilitation stops to discuss the critical item altogether. In this way, the easily defined items get through the process without necessarily involving everybody, speeding up the clarification process.

## 1-2-4-All

This technique, popularized by the Liberating Structure[282] community, aims to engage everyone simultaneously in generating questions, ideas, and suggestions. It consists of four time-boxes, as follows:

- **Alone.** Everybody read the PBI and reflect on it

---

[282]https://www.liberatingstructures.com/1-1-2-4-all/

- **Pairs**. Everybody discuss with another person which elements need to be clarified and specified
- **Four**. Pair of Pairs put the questions they discussed together
- **All**. Each group of four, in turn, asks one question from their list, and the answers are noted in the PBI.

The original format time-box, coming from brainstorming and not from Agile Events, propose one minute for Alone, two minutes per Pairs, four minutes for the group of Four, and five minutes for the ALL. I found this time-box too short, so I used:

- **Alone**: 1 minute
- **Pairs**: 5 minutes
- **Four**: 10 minutes
- **All**: as needed, within the total event time-box

I recommend experimenting with the time box duration since it depends on the context and cannot be generalized.

## Value Poker

This technique aims to facilitate a rich conversation about the value of alternatives. Depending on the situation, it might be alternative features of a product, competing projects, alternative niche markets or use cases, etc.

A mix of different approaches inspires this technique; at the moment I am writing this chapter, I couldn't find another source facilitating it the same way I do it, so it might be a naive way I adapted over time. However, the Excel templates of this technique are available on the Download Section[283] of my website.

The technique starts with a stakeholder spreadsheet containing the list of features and a budget to spend on them. Then, every

---

[283]https://paolo.sammiche.li/download

stakeholder is requested to spend their budget entirely, calculated by multiplying the number of options by 30. In the example, we have ten features, so the budget is 300; if we had twelve features, it would have been 360.

## VALUE POKER

| Area | Feature | Value | BUDGET | 300 | | LEGEND | |
|------|---------|-------|--------|-----|--|--------|--|
| Area 1 | Feature 1 | | TOTAL | 0 | | 0 | No Value |
| | Feature 2 | 0 | LEFTOVER | 300 | | 10 | Very Low Value |
| | Feature 3 | 10 | | | | 20 | Low Value |
| Area 2 | Feature 4 | 20 | | | | 30 | Average Value |
| | Feature 5 | 30 | | | | 40 | High Value |
| | Feature 6 | 40 | | | | 50 | Very High Value |
| | Feature 7 | 50 | | | | | |
| Area x | Feature 8 | | | | | | |
| | Feature 9 | | | | | | |
| | Feature 10 | | | | | | |

I usually send this file to each stakeholder and ask them to spend their budget entirely buying the Features with amounts ranging from 0 to 50. Then, when I have the files from everybody, I merge them in the "Aggregated VPoker.xlsx" file, and I schedule a meeting with all the stakeholders.

## VALUE POKER

| Area | Feature | SH1 | SH2 | SH3 | SH4 | SH5 | TOT | NOTES | | SH1 | 300 |
|------|---------|-----|-----|-----|-----|-----|-----|-------|--|-----|-----|
| Area 1 | Feature 1 | 20 | 10 | 20 | 30 | 20 | 100 | | | SH2 | 300 |
| | Feature 2 | 50 | 40 | 50 | 50 | 50 | 240 | | | SH3 | 300 |
| | Feature 3 | 50 | 50 | 50 | 40 | 50 | 240 | Priority is NOT obtained | | SH4 | 300 |
| Area 2 | Feature 4 | 20 | 40 | 20 | 30 | 20 | 130 | ordering by this column but | | SH5 | 300 |
| | Feature 5 | 20 | 10 | 10 | 10 | 30 | 80 | using techniques like | | | |
| | Feature 6 | 20 | 10 | 10 | 10 | 20 | 70 | Moscow, Kano, etc., and with | | | |
| | Feature 7 | 20 | 50 | 30 | 30 | 20 | 150 | the information from the | | | |
| Area x | Feature 8 | 10 | 10 | 50 | 20 | 10 | 100 | conversation. | | | |
| | Feature 9 | 50 | 40 | 20 | 30 | 30 | 170 | | | | |
| | Feature 10 | 40 | 40 | 40 | 50 | 50 | 220 | | | | |

At the beginning of this Value Poker meeting, I show the aggregated file (I avoid showing it before to avoid side conversations outside the meeting), and I ask them questions for each feature. If there are opposite values (like somebody said "Very High Value" and somebody else "Very Low Value"), I ask to share pieces of information (or facts) that support this evaluation. I don't try to make them converge on a single evaluation but share as much information as possible. I bring a note taker with me to speed up this process, often the SM of a team.

After reviewing all the features, we close the event, highlighting that the final prioritization will be determined by comparing the value of each element with the effort and using other product management techniques to have a holistic view of the business value.

The benefit of this technique is that it provides a numerical result and a rich set of evidence and facts. In addition, not making the stakeholders converge on a single vote speed up the process and makes it very useful when you find conflicting stakeholders and strong personalities.

Alternative/Similar approaches on this topic you might want to explore are:

- Buy-a-Feature[284]
- 100 Points Method[285]
- The Product Tree Prioritization Framework[286]

# Example of a Scaled AI Development Team

Before describing this example, I would like to stress that every time there's an example or a case study in literature, it is necessarily a snapshot of a system that evolved continuously. I often call it a "single photogram of a long movie." The scenario I am about to explain did not start as depicted and didn't have all the elements introduced simultaneously. In reality, it evolved in a period of more than two years, moving from one to two and then three teams.

---

[284]https://medium.com/left-travel/product-prioritization-buy-a-feature-b5e0caeb25e5
[285]https://www.visual-paradigm.com/scrum/scrum-100-points-method/
[286]https://lazaroibanez.com/the-product-tree-prioritization-framework-d7ab0beff99c

# Context

A leading pharmaceutical company intended to build a "**Natural Language Processing**" platform, to navigate, understand and leverage the exponentially growing collection of unstructured text. The capabilities included typical NLP features like sentiment analysis, topics detection, translation, summarization, and others. The development started with one team building a pilot for a specific use case. Then they involved me as a Scrum@Scale Coach in the process of scaling up to a multi-use-case application with multiple teams.

# Product Architecture

To better scale-up we introduce a modular software architecture. The first iteration had a layered architecture that limited the opportunity of refactoring the product and the organization. While coaching them with the topics described previously, I used the metaphor of an electric car, showing them an old video of Faraday Future's Variable Platform Architecture[287].

With the idea that the *Automatically Enriched Data* is a General Purpose Technology, just like electricity in the Second Industrial Revolution, we identified three modules:

- Vehicle - the users' visible part
- Batteries - where the enriched data is maintained and accessible
- Engine - where the data is enriched

I like this metaphor a lot because, in electric cars, the batteries power the engine and the vehicle, but the engine chargeback the batteries in deceleration. This bi-directional relationship sounded like the process of AI model training (batteries powering the engine)

---

[287]https://youtu.be/SAXoVSXnNTg

and dataset enrichment (engine charging back the batteries). A clever UX designer from the team had the idea of visualizing the modules on a Canvas to facilitate the User Stories' clarification and design. Following a re-elaboration of the original artifact for generic use[288].

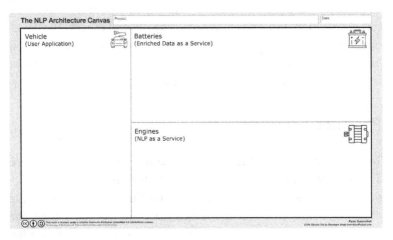

So, why do we consider these three parts of the architecture to be modules and not components?

- Each one could have its users, and we could combine a different set of Batteries and Engines to serve other Vehicles.
- Vehicle could also represent existing applications and not only new AI-specific developments. At the same time, Batteries and Engines could be internal developments of external tools, defined only by their interface.
- Development and Lifecycle were expected to be different; we hypothesize the eventuality of rebuilding a module without significantly changing the others.

---

[288]The ML Architecture Canvas PDF is available to download at https://paolo.sammiche.li/download

## Organizational Architecture

We decided to form the team following the Self-Selecting Team[289] Pattern:

> The worst team dynamics can be found in appointed teams
>
> Therefore
>
> Create enthusiastic teams by letting people select their own teams.

We brainstormed with all the developers the possible scenarios of multiple teams working on the same application, drawing the Team Skill Matrix for each design to discuss the pros and cons of every option. The following picture shows an example of the organizational scenarios we draw before asking teams to form.

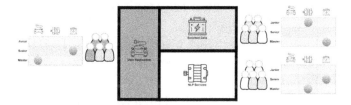

## Calendar

The Product Owner Team decided to have two MetaScrum and two Product Backlog Refinements every Sprint. We also introduced a short meeting to plan the Sprint Review. We slightly changed the timing and the time-boxes during the two years. First, we changed the Sprint Review time to accommodate people connecting from

[289]http://www.orgpatterns.com/Organizational-Patterns-of-Agile-Software-Developm/bookoutline/thepatternlanguages/organizationdesignpatterns/piecemealgrowthpatternlanguage/selfselectingteam

different time zones. Then we also changed the beginning of the Sprint to create more space from the weekend. The following is not an exact picture of their schedule today but an example of how we would probably set our meeting schedule if we did the same project again.

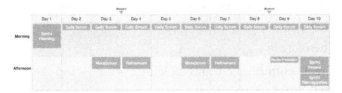

# MetaScrum

At the MetaScrum participates representative from business and development:

- one representative from each development team, typically one person, so three in total
- the entire Product Owner Team (composition varied from six people to four during the two years)
- the Chief Product Owner
- the Scrum Master (we ranged from two to one)
- key stakeholders by invitation.

Every meeting, we had around ten people each time. To deem an item "Good," we established the following guiding question for our "Definition of Good":

- How will this story contribute to the Product Vision and its value?
- Is there any obvious way of splitting it?
- Is the priority of this agreed upon within the Product Owner Team?

- Is this story clear enough within the Product Owner Team?
- Did the MetaScrum vote if it's good enough to take this into the Refinement? (thumbs up/down)

## Sprint Review

Given the diversity of our audience, from business to science, from managers to technical, we decide to group the Sprint Review topics. We start showing the business and end-to-end features first, and then after one short break where business and scientific stakeholders usually leave, we demonstrate the more technical topics.

To collect feedback from everybody, we used a polling tool called Mentimeter[290]. Furthermore, to make the Sprint Review more engaging, we also experimented with the World Café[291] format where there are multiple demos at the same time in breakout rooms, and small stakeholders groups are rotated in all the breakout rooms.

---

[290]https://www.mentimeter.com
[291]https://theagileway.co.za/2019/04/25/world-cafe-retrospective/

# Going into Production

**As the** Author
**I want** to describe production challenges and MLOps
**So that** the reader understands continuous delivery
with AI.

Moving from a PoC running on a development environment to a
production system is always a challenge, for any kind of software.
With AI, we have more additional difficulties on top of the traditional software challenges. According to Andrew NG[292], building
a PoC on a Jupyter notebook is 5/10% of the effort compared with
the remaining effort needed to release it in production[293]; one of his
notable quotes is the following:

> «The job of a machine learning engineer would be much
> simpler if the only thing we ever had to do was do well
> on the holdout test set»

A Production system must run nonstop, at the minimum cost, while
producing the maximum performance. And a system with these
characteristics might be significantly different from the one you
initially developed in a Jupyter notebook.

---

[292]https://en.wikipedia.org/wiki/Andrew_Ng
[293]Introduction to Machine Learning in Production - Andrew NG, DeepLearning.AI

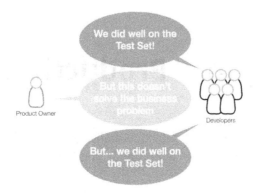

**Unfortunate conversation in many teams**

# AI Development Lifecycle

Let's see the Lifecycle of a generic AI development, without entering too much into the details of the different kinds of systems.

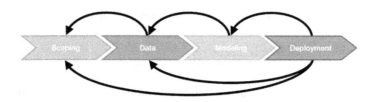

**AI Development Lifecycle**

To develop a machine learning system and take it to production, you will encounter an iterative, non-linear process. You start with **Scoping**, where we define the product's or project's business goal and outcomes. In addition to the general Product Owner's good practices, it would be helpful at this moment to collect, if possible, the HLP (Human Level Performance) of the task we aim to automate. I often heard business stakeholders asking for 95% accuracy when they see an 85% accuracy on a model, just to raise the bar, that would mean nothing without considering the equivalent accuracy of a human being. This kind of request from business people irritates developers a lot since it doesn't come from an understanding of the underlying complexity of the problem.

After Scoping, you focus on **Data**. Working on Data means defining and establishing a baseline, in some cases labeling, and certainly organizing and improving the data. The main concerns usually are consistency and normalization. In academic work, AI developers tend to hold the data fixed and vary the Model (code and hyperparameters) to perform better. However, in a business environment, where your goal is to build and deploy a valuable working machine learning system, AI developers found it more effective to keep the code fixed and focus on optimizing the data and sometimes the hyperparameters. Andrew NG has popularized this latter approach as **Data-Centric AI Development**[294]. Useful techniques in this space are Data Augmentation, where you artificially create more data elaborating the existing ones (for example, in imaging recognition, adding different angles, varying the exposure, and adding noise to the existing images helps the Model to generalize better.) And sometimes, digging into the data produces feedback to scope, which might be bad news, so a redefinition of the business expectation, or good news like new opportunities.

So you have a ready data set, it's time to think about the **Modeling**. This part means selecting and training the Model, performing error analysis, and normally requires numerous loops between Data and Modeling. The recommendation is to start early with a reasonable algorithm, often looking for open-source implementations and a manageable quantity of data. Then iterate quickly, improving the Model and adding more data over time. A reasonable algorithm with good data often outperforms a great algorithm with no-so-good data[295], so iterating between data and modeling is key. There's the challenge of the traceability of this experimentation.

---

[294]A Chat with Andrew on MLOps: From Model-centric to Data-centric AI
[295]Introduction to Machine Learning in Production - Andrew NG, DeepLearning.Al

The principle is that we want to have the reproducibility of each experiment. Many use Experiment Tracking tools like Weight and Biases[296], Comet[297], MLFlow[298], Sage Maker Studio[299], Neptune.ai[300], and others.

Finally, it's time for the **Deployment** into production. This includes also Monitoring and Maintaining the system up and running. Suppose the deployment target is significantly different from the development, like in the case of mobile and IoT applications. In that case, the performance and resource utilization at the serving time will be essential. So, also this step will see multiple iterations back to data and modeling to improve and tune the system to match the desired characteristic in the production environment. Finally, you have your Model working in production. Will it keep performing well? Can the data and the reality that we tried to model change in the future? Also, is your Model robust, secure, or discriminating against minorities? The cycle from production to further improvements may continue for a long time, so it's essential to consider this effort.

# MLOps

The term MLOps originated inside Google and was defined in 2018 by Kaz Sato[301] at the Cloud Next conference[302], as a rephrase of the DevOps definition:

> MLOps is a Machine Learning engineering culture and practice that aims at unifying ML system development

---

[296]https://wandb.ai/site
[297]https://www.comet.com/site/
[298]https://mlflow.org
[299]https://aws.amazon.com/it/pm/sagemaker/
[300]https://neptune.ai/
[301]https://www.linkedin.com/in/kazunori279/
[302]"What is ML Ops? Best Practices for DevOps for ML", Kaz Sato: https://www.youtube.com/watch?v=_jnhXzY1HCw

(Dev) and ML system operation (Ops). MLOps strongly advocates automation and monitoring at all steps of ML system construction, from integration, testing, and releasing to deployment and infrastructure management

The fundamental difference with traditional software is that ML is not just code; it's code plus data. So, for this reason, another popular definition is[303]:

MLOps is a set of practices that combines Machine Learning, DevOps, and Data Engineering, which aims to deploy and maintain ML systems in production reliably and efficiently

## MLOps Manifesto

For a while, the MLOps broad community discussed online the **MLOps Manifesto**, an idea proposed by a company called Dotscience[304] that ceased to operate in May 2020. Unfortunately, the original webpage[305] is now offline, but at the moment of writing still visible through the google cache and the Internet Archive[306].

Following the original text of the MLOps Manifesto.

«We believe that building and deploying machine learning models should be as easy, fast, and safe as Software Engineering is with DevOps. Some people call this DataOps or MLOps. So here is our humble manifesto:

[303]"ML Ops: Machine Learning as an Engineering Discipline", Cristiano Breuel: https://towardsdatascience.com/ml-ops-machine-learning-as-an-engineering-discipline-b86ca4874a3f

[304]https://www.linkedin.com/company/dotscience/about/

[305]https://dotscience.com/manifesto/

[306]http://web.archive.org/web/20200511193351/https://dotscience.com/manifesto/

To achieve DevOps for ML we need to develop systems which meet the following criteria:

### 1. Reproducible

Reproducibility and productivity are inextricably linked. It's difficult to be productive when different team members can't reproduce each others' work. This is harder in ML than in software because test & training data and metrics need to be versioned alongside the code and environment.

### 2. Accountable

Models that are deployed without full provenance, a record of all the steps taken to create the models, can fail to be compliant and are hard to debug. Maintaining this provenance record manually slows you down and is error-prone, so automated tooling is needed.

### 3. Collaborative

Concurrent collaboration – that is, collaboration without treading on each others' toes – is essential. In ML this is harder than in normal software engineering because collaboration applies to notebooks, data, models, and metrics as well as code.

### 4. Continuous

You're not done when you ship. In order to continue delivering value to the business, models must be retrained and statistically monitored to compensate for model drift due to constant changes in your business environment.»

On the Youtube MLOps.community[307] channel, there's a video[308] of Luke Marsden, former Dotscience CEO, explaining this manifesto as a set of tests to assess the maturity of your MLOps Pipeline.

---

[307]https://www.youtube.com/c/MLOpscommunity
[308]https://www.youtube.com/watch?v=hqxQO7MoQIE

# MLOps Capabilities

The Special Interest Group for MLOps[309] of the Continuous Delivery Foundation[310] distinguishes ML model management from traditional software engineering and suggests the following MLOps capabilities[311]:

- Machine learning and software application delivery cycles unification.
- Machine learning artifacts automated testing (like data validation, ML model testing, and ML model integration testing)
- Agile principles application to machine learning projects.
- ML models development as first-class citizens within CI/CD systems[312]
- Technical debt reduction in machine learning models.
- Independence from languages, frameworks, platforms, and infrastructures.

# Why MLOps is so important

The reality of AI into production is depressing for many. Chris Chapo[313], at that time SVP of data and analytics at Gap Inc[314], reported during the round table at Transform 2019[315] that "only 13% of data science projects actually make it into production." Algorithmia's 2021 enterprise trends in machine learning[316] shows that "only 11% of organizations can put a model into production within a week, and 64% take a month or longer[317]" and "the time

---

[309]https://github.com/cdfoundation/sig-mlops

[310]https://cd.foundation

[311]"Machine Learning Operations, Getting started", INNOQ: https://ml-ops.org/#gettingstarted

[312]CI/CD stands for Continuous Integration and Continuous Delivery

[313]https://www.linkedin.com/in/chrischapo/

[314]https://www.gap.com

[315]https://venturebeat.com/ai/transform-2019-lifting-the-hood-on-the-ai-tech-you-need-to-know-about/

[316]https://info.algorithmia.com/hubfs/2020/Reports/2021-Trends-in-ML/Algorithmia_2021_enterprise_ML_trends.pdf

[317]2021 enterprise trends in machine learning, page 23.

required to deploy a model is increasing year-on-year[318]", with companies that require more than a quarter moved from 25% to 40% between 2020 and 2021. Also, the 2021 analysis shows that 38% of organizations spend more than 50% of their data scientists' time on deployment[319], which worsens with scale.

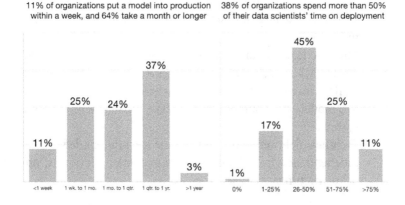

11% of organizations put a model into production within a week, and 64% take a month or longer

38% of organizations spend more than 50% of their data scientists' time on deployment

Findings from "2021 enterprise trends in machine learning"

# Microsoft's Machine Learning operations maturity model

Microsoft's Azure Architecture documentation shows a maturity model to help clarify the Machine Learning Operations principles and practices necessary to run a successful environment.

## Level 0 - No MLOps

It won't be easy to manage a complete machine learning model lifecycle at this level. The teams are disparate, releases are painful,

---

[318]2021 enterprise trends in machine learning, page 24.
[319]2021 enterprise trends in machine learning, page 25.

and most systems exist as "black boxes." Given the lack of transparency, there's little feedback during and after the deployment. On the technology side, we would see:

- Manual software builds and deployments
- Manual model training
- Manual testing of model and application
- No centralized tracking of model performance

## Level 1 - DevOps without MLOps

Here the releases are less painful than on the previous level. Developers rely on Data Scientists for deploying a new model. There's still limited feedback on how well a model performs in production, and it isn't easy to trace and reproduce results. The technology would include the following:

- Automated Software builds
- Automated tests for application code
- Nothing on the ML side

## Level 2 - Automated Training

At this level, the training environment is fully managed and traceable. It is easy to reproduce a model back in time. The production releases are still manual but with relatively low friction. On the technology side, we have the following:

- Automated model training
- Centralized tracking of model performance over time
- Model versioning management

### Level 3 - Automated Model Deployment

Now things start to be smooth; releasing a new model causes low friction and is automatic.
There's full traceability from deployment back to the original data, and the entire environment is managed from Training through Testing until Production. The technology includes:

- Integrated A/B testing of model performance for deployment
- Automated tests for all code
- Centralized tracking of model training performance

### Level 4 - Full MLOps Automated Operations

The system is fully automated and easily monitored at this final level. The production systems provide information on how to improve and, in some cases, automatically improve with new models. Thanks to full automation and continuous monitoring, you can approach a zero-downtime system. The technology now features:

- Automated model training, testing, and deployment
- Verbose, centralized metrics from production
- Continuous monitoring and re-training, when needed

Additional information on the detailed characteristics for all levels of the MLOPS Maturity Model is continuously updated on Microsoft's Azure Architecture documentation[320] page.

## MLOps: continuous delivery and automation pipelines

Google Cloud provided a schematic description of how to adopt MLOps and continuously deliver ML solutions in production with

---

[320]https://learn.microsoft.com/en-us/azure/architecture/example-scenario/mlops/mlops-maturity-model

a fully automated pipeline[321]. This strongly automated Continuous Integration / Continuous Delivery system (CI/CD) allows quick and reliable updates of the production pipelines. With the help of an automated CI/CD solution, data scientists can quickly investigate novel feature engineering, model architecture, hyperparameter, and deploy them to the target environment automatically. The implementation of the ML pipeline utilizing CI/CD, which combines the features of an automated ML pipeline setup with automated CI/CD procedures, is shown in the diagram below.

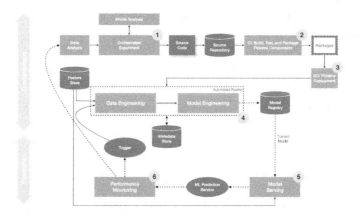

The pipeline consists of the following stages, shown in the above schema with the numbers from 1 to 6:

1. **Development and experimentation.** The output is the source code for pipelines: Data extraction, validation, preparation, model training, model evaluation, model testing
2. **Pipeline continuous integration.** The output is the pipeline components to be deployed: packages and executables.
3. **Pipeline continuous delivery.** The output is the deployed pipeline with the new implementation of the Model.

---

[321]https://cloud.google.com/architecture/mlops-continuous-delivery-and-automation-pipelines-in-machine-learning?hl=en

4. **Automated triggering**. The pipeline is automatically executed in production. Schedule or trigger are used. The output is the trained Model that is stored in the Model registry.

5. **Model continuous delivery**, Model serving for prediction. The output is the deployed Model Prediction Service.

6. **Monitoring**, collecting data about the Model performance on live data. The output is a trigger to execute the pipeline or to start a new experiment cycle.

Similar, with a little bit fewer details, is the diagram provided by Amazon on how SageMaker MLOps[322] works on the AWS environment:

So, to recap, MLOps is an ML engineering culture that includes multiple practices:

- **Continuous Integration (CI)**, extends the testing and validating of code and components by adding testing and validating data and models.
- **Continuous Delivery (CD)**, the delivery of an ML training pipeline that automatically deploys another ML model prediction service.

---

[322]https://aws.amazon.com/sagemaker/mlops/

- **Continuous Training (CT)**, automatically retrains ML models for re-deployment.
- **Continuous Monitoring (CM)**, with monitoring production data and model performance metrics related to business metrics.

## Further Readings

- Machine Learning Operations, INNOQ: https://ml-ops.org
- Awesome MLOps, Larysa Visengeriyeva: https://github.com/visenger/awesome-mlops
- CDF Special Interest Group's MLOps Roadmaps[323]
- Google's Continuous delivery and automation pipelines in machine learning[324]
- Microsoft's Machine Learning operations maturity model[325]

---

[323]https://github.com/cdfoundation/sig-mlops/blob/master/roadmap/
[324]https://cloud.google.com/architecture/mlops-continuous-delivery-and-automation-pipelines-in-machine-learning
[325]https://learn.microsoft.com/en-us/azure/architecture/example-scenario/mlops/mlops-maturity-model

# Coaching Conversations

**As the** Author
**I want** to document practical coaching examples
**So that** people get inspired on how to adopt it in their development.

This book's third part contains interviews and case studies of organizations developing artificial intelligence applications using Scrum and other Agile approaches. Every conversation is typically divided into two parts, where the first one describes the context, the current organization, the results, and the challenges. The second part contains ideas and options to experiment with to improve the organization more.

# Animal Health Application

In January 2022, I interviewed somebody who worked on a project for developing an Animal Health Application. The idea was to create an application to help farmers manage their herds and collect data, with specific sensors, about the animals they were breeding. With the obtained data, they wanted to collect the essential information for efficiency and then leverage it with AI algorithms to get insights to prevent mortality by detecting symptoms of diseases. In this way, they could engage with veterinarians and treat proactive animals, improving the different species' life and increasing the meat quality for the end customers' benefit.

## Context

The initiative was very innovative. Even though it was within a big corporation, the project sounded more like a real startup since it needed to validate assumptions about the needs for such analysis, the customer's tangible benefits, and the business model's viability.

## Organization

The development organization consisted of a single Scrum Team, with a dedicated Product Owner and a Scrum Master. Developers included people with all the necessary skills: UX, Front-End Developers, Back-Front-EndEnd Developers, and a Data Scientist. They sprinted on a two-week cadence, with regular Sprint Reviews and Retrospectives.

# Benefits

This setting saw the usual Scrum Benefits. And thanks to frequent feedback from internal stakeholders, they developed an MVP quickly. After the first MVP lunch, they got a few early adopters, real farmers, that were paying a monthly fee. Some of these early adopters were attending Sprint Reviews providing feedback on usability and needed features. The first MVP, though, was a traditional software application. Initially, the focus was to give clients a tool to manage herd breeding and collect data with specific sensors.

# Challenges

The team experienced internal communication problems since they quickly became a rather big team. The enthusiasm was high after the first MVP release, so the company hired more people. At some point, they went over the Scrum limit of 10 people. In addition, most of them were consultants with a strong emphasis on their development roles; Front-End Developers used to work only on Front End, Back-End Developers only on Back End, etc.

After the initial incubation phase, the release of the MVP, and the first paying customers, the application moved to the corporate environment to become a standard part of the offering. The excitement started to decrease, and some people from the consultancy left, increasing the team's instability. This turnover increased the accumulation of technical debt. In the beginning, the declining code state wasn't clear to everybody. The division between Front-End and Back-End limited the number of eyes around problems, and the problem remained undetected by the Product Owner. Things worsened with the Covid-19 Pandemic when the entire team became remote instead of fully co-located.

The AI part was entirely separated. There was no data to analyze in the early beginning, so the Data Scientist joined the team little bit before the MVP launch. Since he was a single person, he worked alone most of the time. For the rest of the group, the concept was "you use your data voodoo and with your AI magic at some point you will have some insights to show in the application."

Unfortunately, the data didn't contain a strong signal to catch patterns and generate insights regarding mortality prevention. This uncertainty about the model accuracy delayed the beginning of the integration with the rest of the application. For months the Data Science Engineer tried different approaches and requested a different kind of data, but without success. Finally, they attempted to look for "anomalies" in water/food consumption to have an early indication of diseases. This time it was shown to be a more promising approach and finally produced some pieces of evidence on a Jupyter Notebook that convinced the Product Owner.

Here things became complex. The software developers expected the Data Science Engineer to put the model in production by himself, exposing a Rest API. But unfortunately, the Data Science Engineer didn't consider this effort only on his shoulders. This misunderstanding caused the initial friction. When they started discussing the details of this development, the application back end didn't have the architecture in place to send data to a model and get a structured response. And in addition, the software developers were mitigating the technical debt and that was taking more than what they expected, creating additional frictions. Additional people left the team, and the estimates for refactoring the back end and making it able to collect the insights from the model were high and concerned the Product Owner. The farmers were asking instead for more features on the software part to make their life easier in managing the herds.

With the new year, some company managers changed and presented a new business strategy. For the Animal Health project, unfortunately, there was no love anymore. The company's focus and budget got diverted elsewhere, so the AI module of the application never landed in production.

## Learnings

In Retrospect, the most critical improvement would have been a better understanding of the early adopters' point of view. What business cares more about is ROI, which for breeders is the ratio between food costs and animal weight when they sell it. That doesn't mean having the highest possible weight but a specific weight window where the profit is the highest. Focusing only on the features that were taking the clients to match this goal would have increased the chance of success and customer happiness. And together with their satisfaction, the company would have been willing to put more funding into developing more sophisticated features, including AI.

Understanding the quality of the data is critical, even before committing to developing anything related to AI and Data Science.

Educating Product Owners and Software Developers about AI Development would have been essential. However, the reality is that Machine Learning is not a "magic trick." Instead, it only finds the patterns in the data.

Finally, it would have helped to clearly communicate that taking a PoC Model into a production system requires a lot of work. Part of this work is software development, so collaboration between different roles is critical.

# Coaching Conversation

While reflecting on the story of this team during the interview, we browsed the book together. They liked the Mitosis Pattern to prevent their problem of scaling up too fast and becoming a big team with communication problems.

They also found helpful the concept of Modular Architecture in the Agile Architecture principles chapter together with the Machine Learning Canvas.

Another interesting concept was the chapter about Skill Matrix and the idea of rewarding those who also develop horizontal knowledge, not only deep ones.

Finally, with T-Shaped skills and Modular Architecture, it would be beneficial to have two small teams instead of one big team. The team for the AI Models with at least one Back-End developer so that if the AI integration had started earlier, it would have landed in production and learned faster.

# Rasa.com

During an online conference, I met Alan Nichol[326], CTO of Rasa Technologies[327]. I got fascinated by his Agile approach to developing Conversational AI, called **CDD - Conversational Driven Development**, so I started exchanging ideas with him.

## Conversation Driven Development

Rasa Technologies[328] published their method to develop Conversational AI applications, called Conversation Driven Development (CDD). It means listening to your users and using those insights to improve your AI assistant. CDD is composed of 6 actions:

1. **Share:** Give your prototype to users to test as early as possible. People will always surprise you with what they say. Unfortunately, too many teams spend months designing conversations that will never happen.

2. **Review:** Take time to read through people's conversations with your assistant. It's helpful at every project stage, from prototype to production. Unfortunately, too many teams get caught up looking exclusively at metrics (like "what % of users express intent X?").

3. **Annotate:** Improve your NLU model based on messages from real conversations. Coming up with examples yourself or generating synthetic samples with a paraphrasing approach can help you bootstrap. But when you're going into production, less than 10% of your data should be artificial.

---

[326]https://www.linkedin.com/in/anichol/
[327]https://rasa.com
[328]https://rasa.com

4. **Test**: Use whole conversations as end-to-end tests of your assistant. Professional teams don't ship applications without rigorous testing. When you go into production, you should have dozens of end-to-end tests covering the most critical conversations. Then, use continuous integration and deployment to ship updates reliably.

5. **Track**: Come up with a way to identify successful conversations. For example, a user taking action (like signing up for your service) or not taking action (like not getting back in touch with support within 24 hours). Then, use that data to tag and filter conversations to understand what's working and what's not.

6. **Fix**: Study conversations that went smoothly and ones that failed. Successful conversations can become tests right away. Unsuccessful talks show you where you need more training data or where you need to fix your code. Track the different ways your assistant fails so you know you're reducing failures over time.

Alan Nichol[329], CTO of Rasa Technologies[330], explained the reason for the shift of the development approach as follows:

> «the shift to CDD is analogous to switching from waterfall to agile development. In both cases, you cannot anticipate what's ahead, so it's better to lean into that uncertainty and build an iterative process. Agile is necessary because you can't plan ahead for how long every feature will take to build. CDD is necessary because you can't anticipate all the things users will say to your assistant.»

I love the formulation of CDD, with "Share" as the first step. But, of course, one could argue that the first step should be "Build." The learning is that, contrary to traditional software development, where you develop the software (and you test it) to put it into

---

[329]https://www.linkedin.com/in/anichol/
[330]https://rasa.com

production, with Conversational AI, you put it in production to develop it (and test it). Kudos to Alan and the people at Rasa for clearly capturing this crucial nuance in the CDD formalization.

# CDD in early stages of development

According to Rasa[331], if you're at the earliest stage of bot development, it might seem like CDD has no role since you have no conversations yet! However, there are CDD actions you can take at the very beginning of bot development with Rasa:

1. See the best practices for NLU data[332] and Stories[333] for details on creating training data with CDD in mind.
2. Give your bot to test users early on. CDD is all about listening to your users, so the earlier you find some, the better. Test users can be anyone who doesn't already know how your bot works from the inside. People on the bot development team should not be test users since they know exactly what the bot can and can't do. Don't overinstruct your test users; they should have only as much knowledge of the bot's domain as your end users will have.
3. Set up a CI/CD pipeline[334]. CDD leads to frequent, minor updates to your bot as you gather insights from bot conversations. Setting up a CI/CD pipeline early in development will enable you to act quickly on what you see in conversations.

Once your bot is in production[335], you'll have more conversations to gain insights. Then you can fully apply CDD actions. At this stage,

---

[331]https://rasa.com/docs/rasa/conversation-driven-development/#cdd-in-early-stages-of-development
[332]https://rasa.com/docs/rasa/generating-nlu-data/
[333]https://rasa.com/docs/rasa/writing-stories
[334]https://rasa.com/docs/rasa/setting-up-ci-cd
[335]https://rasa.com/docs/rasa/conversation-driven-development/#cdd-with-a-bot-in-production

you can install Rasa Enterprise[336] on a server to both deploy your bot and enable CDD with a bot in production.

# Further readings

- Conversation-Driven Development[337] Page
- Rasa.com[338] Website

---

[336]https://rasa.com/docs/rasa-enterprise/installation-and-setup/installation-guide/#helm-chart

[337]https://rasa.com/docs/rasa/conversation-driven-development/

[338]https://rasa.com

# Tiledesk.com

In September 2022, I interviewed Michele Pomposo, COO of Tiledesk[339]. The company, operating since 2020, develops an Open Source AI conversational platform for customer engagement from lead generation to post-sales.

It is composed of two main components:

- Tiledesk Live Chat Widget[340]
- Tiledesk Chatbot[341]

The **Live Chat** solution provides an integrated platform to manage customer service and engagement activities with many operators to answer customer requests on multiple channels and projects simultaneously. The available channels include Web Chat on popular Content Management Systems like WordPress, Drupal, Joomla, Prestashop, and Shopify. In addition, many instant message channels are supported, such as WhatsApp, Facebook Messenger, Telegram, Email, and others[342].

The Tiledesk **ChatBot** can feature Tiledesk Live Chat with an AI solution that automates simple requests with a Conversational AI and also integrates other Chatbot solutions such as Rasa[343] and Google DialogFlow[344]. Furthermore, with Tiledesk, it's easy to integrate other knowledge systems or build a new one from scratch to enhance the performance of the Tiledesk ChatBot.

---

[339]https://tiledesk.com
[340]https://tiledesk.com/free-live-chat-widget/
[341]https://tiledesk.com/no-code-chatbot-builder/
[342]https://tiledesk.com/integrations-live-chat/
[343]https://rasa.com
[344]https://cloud.google.com/dialogflow

The company is focused on developing a No-Code Open Source Chatbot builder that will allow the design of conversational applications and chatbots without writing a single line of code.

# Context

The company employs about ten people, of which seventy percent are developers. Although they are still a startup, at the moment of the interview, they closed the first round of investments for 600k euros [345]. They offer on-cloud and on-premise solutions and have clients across Europe, the US, South America, and Asia, from fast-growing startups to global brands.

# Organization

The development cycle follows a flow structure; they don't have regular sprints but a continuous flow of features, with the Lean one-piece-flow approach, typical in companies following the Open-Source development model. All the developments are on the public GitHub and released as Open Source with the MIT License[346].

---

[345] https://tiledesk.com/2022/05/15/tiledesk-free-live-chat-announces-its-first-funding-round/

[346] https://opensource.org/licenses/MIT

## Test-driven Development and Continuous Integration

The production infrastructure is based on a Kubernetes[347] cluster hosted on Google Cluster Platform[348]. Delivery in production is not automated, while they heavily automate testing and integration activities. Thanks to their open-source DNA and being fully hosted on GitHub, they heavily take advantage of GitHub Actions[349] for DevOps. For automated testing, they use CircleCI[350]. Docker[351] images building for every single component automatically published on Docker Hub is delegated to GitHub Actions. Tiledesk deploys each component as Docker images. Still, due to the number of components that compose the whole Tiledesk-stack, the images are available for "fast-starting" with a Docker-compose distribution file[352]. For installation on the Kubernetes clusters, they also use Helm[353] files.

## MLOps

Testing of models (algorithms) is performed with isolated sandboxes of the tiledesk-ai project before pushing those models into production.
The principal AI features are training of the models, intent classification, and entity extraction. These capabilities are realized thanks to a corpus of data obtained by anonymized Tiledesk conversations. Models' testing is done with the Python Pytest library. Testing guarantees enabling automated bias detection.
CircleCI[354] continuously automates testing and modeling. Furthermore, at the moment of the interview, they are evaluating if/when creating Docker images for the models.

---

[347]https://kubernetes.io
[348]https://en.wikipedia.org/wiki/Google_Cloud_Platform
[349]https://github.com/features/actions
[350]https://circleci.com
[351]https://www.docker.com
[352]https://github.com/Tiledesk#how-to-install-tiledesk
[353]https://helm.sh
[354]https://circleci.com

## Task management

The work is organized in a Kanban Board[355] with columns containing:

- **New**, with the new ideas not yet discussed and prioritized
- **Backlog**, with the items committed to the development
- **Ready**, with the clarified items
- **In progress**, with all the work-in-progress items
- **Review**, containing all the items that need to be reviewed
- **Done**, with items approved and committed to the main trunk of the code.

Task assignment is not an issue, given the current structure where most people work only on one component, and there is a 1:1 relationship between the developer and components. In addition, the development cycle is organized without a fixed cadence, and the COO admits that sometimes it is skipped. The company leadership, though, meets in presence with a monthly cadence; any other activity instead is performed remotely.

# Benefits

The current nimble and simple structure allows new ideas to be developed quickly, maintaining low operating costs. A recent example is WhatsApp integration: Meta released the public APIs at the

---

[355]https://en.wikipedia.org/wiki/Kanban_board

end of May 2022, and Tiledesk released its WhatsApp integration before the end of August. Furthermore, thanks to the Open Source Model, the contributors' community, launched in July 2022, quickly reached more than 100 active members on the Discord[356] Channel from all around the world in less than two months[357]. At the moment of the interview, the Tiledesk solution has more than 10 thousand downloads on Docker Hub.

## Challenges

Even though having a clear maintainer for each module makes coordination very easy, since anybody knows who to ask questions for each component, this structure provides zero resilience. The COO admits that this initial structure will need further solidification as soon as the company grows. Serving corporate clients is challenging with a few developers, and a more regular cadence would help many aspects, and also the marketing strategy. He also notices the firefighting tendency to become dominant.

## Coaching Conversation

Michele previously worked on a company I helped transform toward Agility, so he knows all the benefits of a Scrum organization. We discussed the topics of regular releases, continuous integration, and MLOps. We also briefly compared the evolution I've seen of the Ubuntu project when it became more prominent. One idea he liked was to organize a regular Developer Summit. We decided to meet again when the company grows in the number of employees.

---

[356]https://discord.com
[357]https://tiledesk.com/open-source-community/

# Appendix

**As the** Author
**I want** to have additional material
**So that** the reader gets more value with this book.

In this last part, you will find additional material about Business Agility in general that I found helpful in Artificial Intelligence projects. The chapters about Popcorn Flow, Agile Management, How to Interview the Scrum Master, and Cynefin comes from my previous book, "Scrum for Hardware," since they were a great compendium also in Manufacturing.

# Popcorn Flow

In this chapter, you find the interview with Claudio Perrone[358], author of Popcorn Flow[359], where he explains his method.

## Hi Claudio, thanks for your time. Let's start with the most obvious question: What is PopcornFlow?

PopcornFlow is a method to introduce, sustain, and accelerate continuous innovation & change. It promotes ultra-rapid experimentation to make better decisions under uncertainty.

It consists of two parts: a decision cycle and a set of principles.

Most people come across PopcornFlow through its 7-step decision cycle. No surprises there, as the word *Popcorn* stands for the initials of each step:

---

[358]https://www.linkedin.com/in/claudioperrone/
[359]https://popcornflow.com/

- Problems and observations
- Options
- Possible experiments
- Committed
- Ongoing
- Review
- Next

Teams and individuals reason about the problems they face, options to neutralize or reduce the impact of those problems, and possible experiments to explore one or more of those options. Either just-in-time or on a fast cadence, they capture the details on sticky notes and place them on a PopcornFlow board - a visual board that represents each step as a column. They then *flow* experiments through the board, bringing to the surface (what I call) a *learning stream*. I often work with small teams where we co-design several experiments per week.

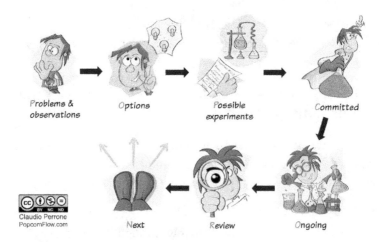

Problems &          Options          Possible          Committed
observations                          experiments

Claudio Perrone
PopcornFlow.com          Next          Review          Ongoing

The decision cycle reveals only part of the story - the machinery. The secret to unleashing PopcornFlow lies in its guiding principles:

1. If change is hard, make it continuous (The Virus Principle).

2. It's not only what you do but also what you learn by doing it that matters (The Ladder Principle).
3. Everybody is entitled to their own opinion, but a shared opinion is a fact (The Freedom Principle).
4. It's not "fail fast, fail often." It's "learn fast, learn often" (The Skateboarder Principle).
5. Small bets, big win. (Note: The wording of this last principle is still a work in progress, but it's based on Nassim Taleb's concept of "option asymmetry." In a nutshell, it's not about how frequently we meet or exceed our expectations. It's rather about how to limit the cost of each experiment and how much we gain when we are - even if occasionally - right.)

## How was PopcornFlow born?

I love origin stories!

I struggled to come to terms with the debacle of my latest entrepreneurial adventure when Eric Ries took the startup world by storm. He observed that startups operate under extreme uncertainty conditions and promoted a sort-of scientific approach to validate assumptions and converge to a viable business model. The Lean Startup movement was born. Right away, I fiddled with those ideas, both for my own projects and for my clients - many of which were, in fact, fast-growing startups. As I needed to track experiments systematically, I created many Kanban board designs, which admittedly ranged from borderline simplistic to overly complex.

At a conference in Boston, however, something magical happened: Jeff Anderson[360] took the stage to show how he applied Lean Startup concepts to organizational change. He called this Lean Change[361], an approach that was later forked and popularized by Jason Little[362]. Jeff argued that people react to change is highly contextual and

[360]https://www.linkedin.com/in/thomasjeffreyandersontwin/
[361]https://leanpub.com/leanchangemethod
[362]https://leanchange.org/

unpredictable ways. As a result, a team of change agents involved in any large organizational transformation inevitably faces extreme uncertainty conditions - a situation analogous to a startup. Wow, that was a smashing realization! It was early days, and the session was hotly debated. I chatted with Jeff right afterward. Frankly, neither the scenario Jeff had described at the time - an appointed team of change agents experimenting *on* change recipients - nor most of the implementation details felt quite right. But it didn't matter: I realized I could devote my efforts and tools to co-design experiments and negotiate change *with* people in organizations.

I wasted no time. Back in Europe, a startup urged me to help them address a critical situation to their survival. Their (anything-but) Scrum development team had been unable to release software for months due to quality and integration problems. People were distributed across several countries. The most troubling aspect was that the company had outsourced core parts of the platform to a third-party company. Their management had since gone rogue: their lack of transparency and shady tactics had created an unsustainable situation.

With the motto "soft on people, hard on systems," we agreed to go back to basics and resume Scrum. My aim was to put a solid process in place, establish radical transparency, and treat with respect everyone involved in the production line - including the external partners.

I explained that Agile is not about ceremonies. It's about humility: we don't pretend to know and impose The One True Way to develop software. So, we start with what we know so far and then continuously inspect and adapt our approach. During our weekly retrospectives, we negotiated small change experiments to improve how we worked together. For example, in our communication, the tools we used, how we reviewed our code, and much more. We visually tracked problems and observations - facts but also very personal opinions. We acted on the ones we could agree with (or, at least, not violently disagree with). It was all there for people to see. And so, with little fanfare, PopcornFlow became a natural way to facilitate our Scrum retrospectives.

Every week, I asked these questions:

- What experiments did we agree to do?
- Which one did we actually do?
- What did we expect to happen?
- What did we learn?
- Based on what we learned, what are we going to do next?

Some experiments met our expectations. Others didn't. But as the co-designed experiments entered the cycle, the team's climate improved steadily. Little by little, people's confidence grew. They experimented several times throughout each Sprint. Even one improvement experiment each week would have been enough. Instead, they launched 5 or 6 of those every week - sometimes even 10! It didn't take long for the results to arrive. The company went from being unable to release the product for months to release it several times a day. My job was done.

I saw their PopcornFlow board once again, almost a year later. It had captured hundreds of experiments. Unsurprisingly, as the company grew, other boards had appeared in other parts of the organization, well outside the original development team. Popcorn-Flow had impacted marketing, sales, and strategy.

Then a friend of mine - an Agile coach who had introduced Popcorn-Flow in his organization - suggested: "Claudio, drop everything else and focus on PopcornFlow. This thing is freaking amazing."

So I did.

## What makes PopcornFlow different?

Some practitioners have originally likened the PopcornFlow steps to PDCA/PDSA[363], the well-known Shewhart[364]/Deming[365] cycle. The similarity is only superficial, however. They operate in very different domains of complexity. Like two faces of the same coin, they are opposite and complementary.

With PDSA, we deliberately "go slow to go fast." With PopcornFlow, we "go fast to learn faster." The former is about *continuous improvement*, the latter is about *continuous change*. But above all, PDSA's approach is based on root-cause analysis and the scientific method, PopcornFlow is not! Consider the Freedom Principle I mentioned before, for example. (Don't worry: it has *metaphorical* rather than *literal* meaning.) Subjectivity plays a primary role, and we can exploit it. It doesn't sound very *scientific*, does it?

Over time, I developed a more refined sense of the forces at work and realized that PopcornFlow best operates in complex rather than complicated domains (see Dave Snowden's Cynefin[366] framework). In this context, PopcornFlow problems are, essentially, system *probes*. To a great extent, we use uncontrolled parallel experiments to *explore options* and change the system dynamics. In fact, I even came to question Lean Startup's scientific claims, particularly around the idea of *validated learning*. Is it possible that maybe we are doing the right things for the wrong reasons?

And so, despite its origins, PopcornFlow has changed and evolved into something different. Its decision cycle is, perhaps, a very pragmatic expression of John Boyd's OODA loop[367]; its philosophy echoes Nassim Taleb's Antifragile[368] approach.

---

[363]https://en.wikipedia.org/wiki/PDCA
[364]https://en.wikipedia.org/wiki/Walter_A._Shewhart
[365]https://en.wikipedia.org/wiki/W._Edwards_Deming
[366]https://en.wikipedia.org/wiki/Cynefin_framework
[367]https://en.wikipedia.org/wiki/OODA_loop
[368]https://en.wikipedia.org/wiki/Antifragile

## In which areas have you seen people using PopcornFlow?

My observation is that organizations want to innovate, but they don't know how to do it. PopcornFlow is relatively young and still evolving. Yet, it already found its way in startups, large financial institutions, well-known technology companies, and more. Last year, a group in the Canadian public sector, for example, won two prestigious national innovation awards; the secret - they revealed - was *a magic trick up their sleeve*. I often use PopcornFlow to coach Agile teams and facilitate highly effective retrospectives. Teams trade options outside their immediate circle, too - a crucial mechanism to reduce the inevitable bias. Combined with jobs-to-be-done theory, it also works well for product and service innovation. I'm occasionally called to help sales and marketing teams too. Basically, if you need to introduce change, PopcornFlow may be a good fit. There is nothing intrinsically technological or "corporate" about it. I even use it to negotiate change with my kid (who is at the high-functioning end of the autism spectrum[369]). It's been used by families, job seekers, school teachers, life coaches, psychologists, and more. You see? It's about decisions. And life is full of those.

## What can we expect from PopcornFlow in the future?

Workshops, coaching, and speaking gigs aside, these days, I'm developing a digital platform and writing a book. I am trying hard to keep the technical jargon to a minimum and, hopefully, reach a wider audience. I designed PopcornFlow to be *so simple that even a five-year-old child could understand it*. "This way," I thought, "grown-ups will understand it too." My son became quite proficient at that age, but the jury's still out on some adults. Ah ah.

Interview ©2018 Claudio Perrone, Paolo Sammicheli.

---

[369]https://www.autismspeaks.org/what-autism/asperger-syndrome

# Cynefin

The complexity theory is a widely debated topic in various science branches, and there is no generally defined definition of what **complexity** is. Cynefin[370] is a decision-making framework developed by Dave Snowden within IBM in the early 2000s that provides a concise and straightforward management strategy for each of the domains defined. In addition to being used in IBM, Cynefin is applied to product development, market analysis, supply chain management, branding, customer relationship management, emergency management, and several other critical areas by the government of many countries worldwide. Now, let us examine the Cynefin Framework in greater detail.

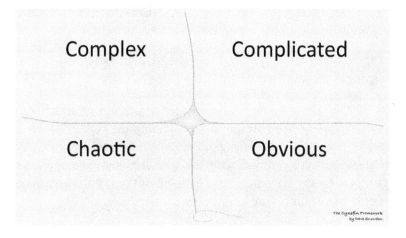

The Cynefin model has four domains (Obvious, Complicated, Complex, Chaotic), represented as four quadrants. It suggests a clear strategy. A fifth domain called Disorder and illustrated in the center

---

[370]https://en.wikipedia.org/wiki/Cynefin_framework

is a situation where there is no clarity about which of the other domains apply.

## Obvious Domain

In the Obvious domain, components are strongly coupled. This is a predictable and understandable domain; knowledge is enough to deal with the issues involved in this spectrum.

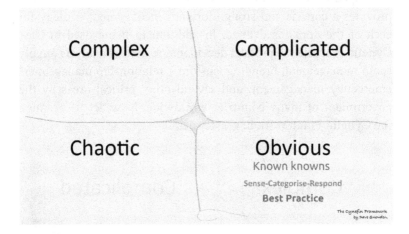

In an Obvious domain, the associated management strategy is **Sense - Categorise - Respond**. Considering the type of problem (Sense), we use our knowledge to recognize its reference category (Categorise) and respond with the best solution (Respond). An Obvious domain is characterized by the Best Practices, where there is only one optimal way to solve the problem.

## Complicated Domain

In the Complicated domain, components are coupled by a cause-effect relationship, but this is not easily understandable. Our expertise is thus not sufficient to address the problem immediately as in the Obvious domains.

In a Complicated domain, the associated management strategy is **Sense – Analyse - Respond**. In other words, realizing the type of issue (Sense), we study it in detail (Analyse) and find the most appropriate response (Respond). A Complicated domain does not have a single optimal solution but several Good Practices. These different methods are equally worth that allows solving the problem effectively.

## Complex Domain

In a Complex domain, interactions between different components are not clearly perceptible a priori.

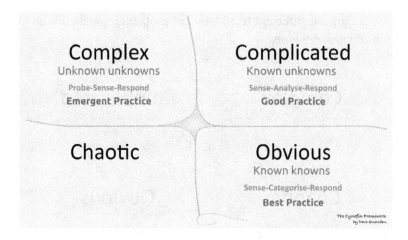

In a Complex domain, we do not know what we do not know (Unknown Unknowns). The management strategy associated with this domain is **Probe - Sense - Respond**. This involves performing an experiment (Probe), observing the results (Sense), and responding accordingly (Respond), probably with a new investigation capable of expanding our knowledge. In this context, the approach is iterative and incremental, and practices are called Emergent Practices precisely because they emerge during the discovery process.

## Chaotic Domain

In the Chaotic domain, it is impossible to know what we do not know (Unknowable Unknowns). An experiment repeated infinitely in a Chaotic domain always produces different results, so it is useless. Studying a Chaotic domain is even more useless.

The management strategy in a Chaotic domain is **Act - Sense - Respond**. In practice, we need to act (Act), understand what happens while we act (Sense), and try to respond quickly (Respond). Fortunately, a Chaotic domain in nature persists for a short time and tends to stabilize towards a Complex domain.

# Disorder

When we do not know the domain we are in, the Cynefin model calls it Disorder. It is represented by the dark area in the center of the diagram. In this area, the belonging domain is by definition challenging to understand. According to Snowden, the way out of this domain is to break down the situation into constituent parts and assign each of the other four domains previously mentioned.

# Conclusions

Cynefin provides a contextual approach advantageous to managers to orient themselves in the growing complexity of today's challenges.

This is a significant change from a cultural perspective. Instead of obsessively trying to predict the future by understanding it, the management must have iterative and incremental processes that allow safe-to-fail experiments that can incorporate learning gained in successive strategic choices.

# Further readings

- A Leader's Framework for Decision Making[371] - Dave Snowden, Mary E. Boone
- Cynefin - Weaving Sense-Making into the Fabric of Our World[372] - Dave Snowden, Zhen Goh

---

[371]https://hbr.org/2007/11/a-leaders-framework-for-decision-making
[372]https://www.goodreads.com/book/show/55813487-cynefin---weaving-sense-making-into-the-fabric-of-our-world

# Agile Management

An Agile Manager does not do a different job than a traditional manager: like all managers, he *takes difficult decisions.* The difference lies in the way he does it. An Agile Manager has understood and metabolized the concept of complexity, as defined in the Cynefin model, previously described here in the appendix. He needs to "knows not to know." Peter Stevens[373] once told me, "**complicated** is when I know the questions but not the answers, **complex** is when I do not even know the questions". An Agile Manager makes decisions by prioritizing the ability to cope with change. He knows that nothing is definitive, which is why he explores, with the rest of the organization, a world that is a continuous discovery. Agile is a management style closer to the definition of Leadership, and acquiring it requires going through a long and winding path. A list of practical suggestions can be found in the Management 3.0[374] material by Jurgen Appelo[375], of which I reproduce here a small extract.

## Guidelines for Managers in Complexity

1. Address complexity with complexity
2. Use a diversity of perspectives
3. Assume subjectivity and coevolution
4. Steal and tweak
5. Assume dependence on context
6. Anticipate, adapt, explore
7. Reduce the feedback cycle
8. Keep options open

[373]https://www.scrumalliance.org/community/profile/pstevens
[374]https://management30.com/
[375]http://jurgenappelo.com

## Address complexity with complexity

The most complex tool available to you is your brain. To make sense of complex problems, you can use storytelling, metaphors, and visualization tools. **A system's complexity must be adjusted to the complexity of the system it is in,** says Michael R. Lissack in the book "The Interaction of Complexity and Management[376]"

## Use a diversity of perspectives

Complexity per se is an anti-methodology, as opposed to the concept of the silver bullet, functional in every context, which instead the methodologies tend to propose.
Combining a set of different perspectives, even if not perfectly positioned, produces a better point of view than a single well-defined point of view. This is the purpose, for example, of the collaboration between the Product Owner, who has a business focus, with the Development Team, which has a technical focus, in the Scrum Team itself with a single objective.

## Assume subjectivity and coevolution

Complex systems are often also adaptive: their complexity is intrinsic and due to a natural and unpredictable evolution of the system. In this context, the observer influences the observed system, just as the system, in turn, affects the observer. When cause and effect are interdependent, one can solve a situation even by focusing on another.

## Steal and tweak

Successful systems spend much of their time copying and adapting ideas from others. Innovation is often imagined as a process of

---

[376]https://www.goodreads.com/book/show/4852736-the-interaction-of-complexity-and-management

creating new things from scratch; usually, however, invention passes from the transposition of a good idea from one domain to another or from an unprecedented combination of existing ideas.

## Assume dependence on context

Be skeptical: it is not sure that what worked in the past or for other functions will work today for you too. "Any relationship that anyone identifies between a management action and an obtained result may have more to do with time and place than with the action itself," says Ralph Stacey, for example in the book "Complexity and Organizational Reality[377]".

## Anticipate, adapt, explore

Explore a situation by imagining improvements (anticipate), trying something (explore), and responding to the change you get (adapt). In the book "The Toyota Way[378]" we read, in fact, "An evolving and improving system requires by its nature a continuous experimentation".

## Reduce the feedback cycle

"The only way to win is to learn faster than others," says Eric Ries in the book "The Lean Startup[379]". Systems that have a slower feedback loop have a higher extinction rate. It is necessary to iterate every day faster and faster.

## Keep options open

In the book The Interaction of Complexity and Management[380], we read, "The absorption of complexity involves creating risk hedging

---

[377]https://www.goodreads.com/book/show/9927574-complexity-and-organizational-reality
[378]https://www.goodreads.com/book/show/161789.The_Toyota_Way
[379]https://www.goodreads.com/book/show/10127019-the-lean-startup
[380]https://www.goodreads.com/book/show/4852736-the-interaction-of-complexity-and-management

options and strategies", even outside your expectations. Get ready for any kind of surprise.

## In Detail

Another aspect to take into consideration is the ability of systems theory[381]. We need to make decisions that involve and consider the whole system to avoid actions that locally appear to be good but that do not improve, or in the worst cases, degrade the performance at the system level. Peter Senge extensively explores this theme, for example, in the book "The fifth discipline[382]".

# Further readings

Agile management's topic is extensive, and a complete discussion is beyond the scope of this book. Those who wish to further explore the subject are advised to read the following:

- The Leader's Guide to Radical Management: Reinventing the Workplace for the 21st Century[383] - Stephen Denning
- The Fifth Discipline: The Art & Practice of The Learning Organization[384] - Peter Senge
- Management 3.0: Leading Agile Developers, Developing Agile Leaders[385] - Jurgen Appelo
- The Interaction of Complexity and Management[386] - Michael Lissack
- Complexity and Organizational Reality[387] - Ralph D. Stacey

---

[381]https://en.wikipedia.org/wiki/Systems_theory
[382]https://en.wikipedia.org/wiki/The_Fifth_Discipline
[383]https://www.goodreads.com/book/show/8873049-the-leader-s-guide-to-radical-management
[384]https://www.goodreads.com/book/show/255127.The_Fifth_Discipline
[385]https://www.goodreads.com/book/show/10210821-management-3-0
[386]https://www.goodreads.com/book/show/4852736-the-interaction-of-complexity-and-management
[387]https://www.goodreads.com/book/show/9927574-complexity-and-organizational-reality

# How to interview the Scrum Master

The selection of the Scrum Master is not defined anywhere in the Scrum Guide. Who chooses him? With which criteria?

Different methods can be observed: in some cases, the Scrum Master offers voluntarily and is then appointed by the management; in others, he was born as a member of the Team and is elected within it, and often partly continues to carry out development activities, as a team member.

At the beginning of 2018, one of my clients needed to reorganize the development department to harmonize his teams. His Scrum Masters, elected among the team members, carried out their part-time role and continued to work on development as well. Various problems were emerging: in some teams, there was an overabundance of aspiring Scrum Masters while in others, the role had been played by the person with more seniority of service, without however manifesting a great enthusiasm. Playing a role partially also reduced the focus. It provided an alibi for not devoting time to the study of coaching practices.

I suggested taking advantage of the reorganization to experiment with a different method of choosing the Scrum Master, taking inspiration from Craig Larman's LeSS method.

Considering the existing constraint, which required maintaining the number of people employed (*headcount*), Scrum Master would become a full-time assignment. Each Scrum Master would be assigned to two teams. Those wishing to become Scrum Masters should apply to an internal Job Posting and pass an assessment interview held by the Coaches who led the transformation. After that, the teams would indicate their preferences among the selected people. The management would finalize the pairings, trying to satisfy as many people as possible.

The idea of having full-time and professionalized Scrum Masters convinced everyone in the company, and the managers decided to experiment with this different method. The top management assured me that Scrum Master would be a role and not a *job title*. With the mantra "Job and Salary safety, Role unsafety," the new organization was announced to the whole company development department.

## Selection Criteria

I began to think about what could be the way to select candidates. Scrolling back to the book by Lyssa Atkins "Coaching Agile Teams"[388] I pondered on the multiplicity of roles that the Agile Coach must play, and in particular on its three main functions:

- Trainer
- Facilitator
- Coach

I also had a look at "Succeeding with Agile" by Mike Cohn[389] with his acronym *ADAPT*, which is about Awareness, Desire, Ability, Practice, and Transfer. I had a crazy intuition: if ADAPT works for organizations, why shouldn't it be suitable for an individual?

Therefore, I tried to place the meaning of each letter within the context of an aspiring Scrum Master:

- Awareness of the role, and of oneself.

---

[388]https://www.goodreads.com/book/show/8337919-coaching-agile-teams
[389]https://www.goodreads.com/book/show/6707987-succeeding-with-agile

- Desire of the role and how they see themselves into the role.
- Ability to read coaching situations.
- Practice. The practical skills as a facilitator.
- Transfer. The ability to transfer concepts, to teach.

This skill *checklist* seemed to cover well the roles of trainer, facilitator, and coach of the book "Coaching Agile Teams"[390].

# The Interview

The interview was held in a dedicated room. With the candidates' permission, it was audio recorded so that the interviewer would not need to take notes during the interview and focus on the candidate.

The **Awareness** component was explored with two questions:

1. What characteristics should a Scrum Master have?
2. What characteristics, among those you have listed, do you think you have, and on which do you think you have to work harder?

For question 1, there were correct and well-documented answers even in the Certified Scrum Master courses, question 2 aimed at understanding how people were aware of the personal growth path required by the role.

For the **Desire** part, the questions were:

3. Why do you want to be a Scrum Master?
4. Think about yourself tomorrow. You are a Scrum Master. What has changed in you, and what do others say about you?

---

[390]https://www.goodreads.com/book/show/8337919-coaching-agile-teams

Question 3 aimed at understanding if the motivation was related to the role, career, and prestige or if it also derived from the presence of soft relational skills, perhaps developed outside of the working context, with hobbies, sports, and voluntary activities. Question 4 sought to explore how the candidates saw themselves in the role; any awareness of the difficulties would be considered favorably.

The **Ability** part was conducted with two situational questions:

5. In a team of four developers, one person always does solo work. Others suffer from this but do not openly say anything. You are their Scrum Master. What will you do?

6. A manager who has not fully understood Scrum enters the team room and complains that a feature he had promised a client has not been completed yet. The relative story has dragged for a further 2 sprints beyond what expected. He alludes to the fact that the Team does not commit itself. You are the Scrum Master, and you are in the room at that moment. What will you do?

These questions evaluated compliance with the Scrum Guide's principles, the quantity, and quality of options that people listed. An approach in line with systemic thinking and complexity, described in in the Appendix, paragraphs Agile Management and Cynefin.

The **Practice** component aimed at evaluating facilitation and visualization capabilities. The candidate was asked to visualize on a flip chart the concepts that were read from a book[391] as if they were dialogues that emerged in a meeting. Like in discussions, the facilitator can intervene to ask a question but cannot monopolize the speech. It was then explained to the candidate that it was not dictation but a way to visualize the key concepts and that they could interrupt the reading by asking questions without exaggerating.

---

[391]In the case described here, I read to the candidates the chapter "The Fourth Industrial Revolution" from my first book "Scrum for Hardware" https://leanpub.com/Scrum-for-Hardware

This test aimed at evaluating the writing, the order, and the use of color.

Finally, for the **Transfer** part, it was asked to explain what Agile was in the first question and how Scrum worked in a second one. The candidate could use the flip chart if he thought it helpful. The questions were always asked in a situational way (e.g., I am a consultant for a foreign branch, I am traveling in development and meeting you. I invite you to explain what Agile means, the term I heard at a meeting the same morning). Moreover, it was assessed how much the answer strove to adapt to the context and vocabulary of the person who posed the question in the imagined situation.

# Evaluation

The evaluation of the candidates' responses was carried out later, listening to the audio recordings and analyzing the photos of the artifacts produced in the Practice and Transfer questions. At first, the critical aspects of the answers were noted. A grade was then assigned on a scale similar to the Italian scholar one, from 4 to 8. A second evaluation tried to harmonize the judgments once all the interviews were listened to have a balanced vote between the candidates. A summary table was then created in which there was a single vote for each individual component of ADAPT. However, the individual grades were not added to get the final ranking; instead, to try to absorb the complexity of the choice of a suitable Scrum Master, those with serious fails were first discarded. Then, the remaining ones were ordered case by case, trying to evaluate the candidate in its entirety and not based on the mere algebraic sum of votes. The goal was to build a list of ordered people to enter the role to select those who had the smallest gap to fill.

# Outcomes

The development department involved in the process had about 100 employees distributed between systems engineers, support groups, and 10 Scrum teams. The goal was to identify 5 Scrum Master candidates.

As stated to the management before starting the interviews, I would consider this process a success if it surprised me. I other words, if the suitable people emerged from it who had not already seemed such since the beginning of the Agile transition. Of the 5 new Scrum Masters selected, two were former developers. They had managed to overcome in the rankings people who acted as Scrum Masters for about two years, despite not having held this role previously. This showed how much potential and hidden talent there were in them. However, many people excluded from the final choice had demonstrated that they had characteristics of suitability, and this was reassuring in the possible future prospect of having to repeat the process for an enlargement of the workforce or in case of refusals. The new Scrum Masters all showed great enthusiasm, and the first feedback after some Sprints are very encouraging. At the time of the writing of this book, beginning of 2021 - three years after the first use of this practice, I used this approach multiple times in different companies, with a total of nearly thirty candidates. I consider this a valuable tool that helped me to identify suitable candidates for the role in several companies. In particular, three times, my assessment showed a not suitability for candidates. Still, they got employed anyway. In all the cases, they showed significant difficulties in entering the role and progressing with the learning.

# Electronic Version

To download the electronic version, in a DRM-Free PDF and EPUB format, follow this link or scan the QRCode:

https://leanpub.com/scrum-ai/c/carta

The link will work up to 31 December 2027.

This page intentionally left blank

www.ingramcontent.com/pod-product-compliance
Lightning Source LLC
Chambersburg PA
CBHW071110050326
40690CB00008B/1182